What people ar

Surfing the Gala

The astrologer's first job is to demystify. The second is to fascinate. Through his insistence on pure craft winning, at every turn, over personal feelings or bias, Barry Goddard achieves just that. An astrological page turner.
Joanna Watters, author of *Astrology for Today* and *Be Your Own Astrologer*

Barry's book is a fascinating journey of ideas and thoughtful perspectives for anyone interested in astrology and life. He speaks from the position of being a long-experienced astrologer, sharing his insights into birth charts, counselling and also the astrology of current events and social-political trends. The author thinks for himself, yet he sheds new light on many of the ideas, conventions and poorly thought-through notions we might hold in astrology and the helping professions. One key message I like is that he advocates good old simple astrology and its depth of interpretative possibility, without needing to resort to complex astrological concepts and techniques. There's a good dose of life wisdom in this book. I found it a stimulating read. It's not one of those books that gets lost in my 'read later' pile of books.
Palden Jenkins, author of *Living in Time*, *The Historical Ephemeris* and *Power Points in Time*

What a wonderful read! I don't know much about astrology but I am very interested in it and with this book, Barry Goddard makes it easy to understand and fun, yet it has a depth to it that I personally appreciate a lot and which can only come from Spirit I suppose...

An honest book that very eloquently talks about the Great Mystery of life and is simultaneously profoundly down-to-earth and practical. This is just a great read for anyone who is curious (to learn more) about astrology, life itself and why we do the things we do. It clearly expresses a love for the Gods (planets), the Mother (earth) and this mysterious human journey we are all on.

Miranda Visser of https://soulcoachings.com/

Surfing the Galactic Highways

Adventures in Divinatory Astrology

Surfing the Galactic Highways

Adventures in Divinatory Astrology

Barry Goddard

MOON BOOKS

Winchester, UK
Washington, USA

JOHN HUNT PUBLISHING

First published by Moon Books, 2022
Moon Books is an imprint of John Hunt Publishing Ltd., No. 3 East Street, Alresford
Hampshire SO24 9EE, UK
office@jhpbooks.net
www.johnhuntpublishing.com
www.moon-books.net

For distributor details and how to order please visit the 'Ordering' section on our website.

Text copyright: Barry Goddard 2021

ISBN: 978 1 80341 010 4
978 1 80341 011 1 (ebook)
Library of Congress Control Number: 2021943913

All rights reserved. Except for brief quotations in critical articles or reviews, no part of this
book may be reproduced in any manner without prior written permission from the publishers.

The rights of Barry Goddard as author have been asserted in accordance with the Copyright,
Designs and Patents Act 1988.

A CIP catalogue record for this book is available from the British Library.

Design: Matthew Greenfield

UK: Printed and bound by CPI Group (UK) Ltd, Croydon, CR0 4YY
Printed in North America by CPI GPS partners

We operate a distinctive and ethical publishing philosophy in
all areas of our business, from our global network of authors to
production and worldwide distribution.

Contents

Preface

I have been writing pieces on astrology for about 20 years, sometimes for magazines, mainly for my blog and for social media*. But I could never bring myself to write a book. What would its theme be? I didn't have one, and all the astrology books I had seen seemed to have one.

Along with Astrology, the other major current running through my life is Shamanism, and during the Covid lockdowns of 2020 I ran two long, experiential courses on the Medicine Wheel. By the end, I realised I had enough material for a book, and one morning in January 2021 I thought dammit, just start writing! Enough of this self-doubt! So I started writing (under a weighty New Moon in Capricorn in the 10th House), and two months later there was a book on the Medicine Wheel. It was like giving birth to myself.

That, I thought, was that, because, of course, I didn't have a 'proper' theme for an astrology book, even though I had probably written half a dozen books' worth of blogs over the years. But then a few weeks later I began to feel an astrology book in me, an offer from the outer planets that could not be politely refused, and I knew I would just have to start writing and see where it went. How exciting. At last!

My approach to astrology is divinatory: that is, my emphasis lies in allowing something – the gods, the spirits, the otherworld – to speak through me. This is where it blends with Shamanism. My spirits (well, some of them) are in the sky, and they began calling to me as a teenager. I did not, however, begin to do readings until my early forties, once I had had the requisite, and lengthy, initiations from those spirits, that didn't at the time seem to have much to do with astrology.

I have to say that I was a bit slow on the uptake with the

1

book-writing. If I do astrology as the spirit moves me, then how could I possibly know in advance exactly what themes I was going to write about in a book? So often the things we see as shortcomings are pointers to our strengths. It was not 'me' that was going to write this book, it was the gods, and my job was to stay close to them and write according to their promptings. And trust that by the end it would all add up to something.

No doubt that will be for the reader to judge. My style is, I hope, engaging, and the content illuminating. I try to stay close to experience, to personal knowledge of what I am talking about. Passing on information, or other people's ideas, doesn't particularly interest me. The book covers the main subjects that have engaged me over the years.

One astrologer commented that I needed to put in more sources to back up what I say. If this was an academic study, she would have been completely right. But when I thought about it, I realised that the sources for what I say are largely myself. I do readings, I observe, I mull things over. And, I like to think, it gives a certain life to what I have to say. Academic I am not!

This book is aimed at anyone who has a little bit of knowledge of astrology upwards. Astrology is one of those subjects that enters your bones, and if it is there, then it is there, however much or however little you know. It is a primordial connection to the sky that many of us feel.

If I had to draw out some central themes of the book, they would be these: the power of astrology to take our breath away, to enchant us, through the eerie synchronicities it reveals between sky events and earth events; its ability, particularly using the outer planets, to guide us through the deep initiatory and transformative experiences that life, if we are willing, offers us; and an affirmation of the intuitive, non-rational means of knowing, that is so central to who we are as humans, but which is undervalued and even denied in our modern age. Happy surfing!

*www.astrotabletalk.blogspot.com. Also www.shamanic freestate. blogspot.com, and UK Astrologers Facebook group.

Chapter 1

The Power of Astrology

On 8 December 2020 in Coventry, UK Margaret Keenan, 90, became the first person in the world (outside trials) to receive a Covid vaccine. At that moment, the Moon was almost directly overhead, with the stars of the constellation Virgo behind. The Sun would not rise for another 90 minutes, so the Moon was visible, presiding over this event. (Note that the 'overhead' point takes the tilt of Earth into account.)

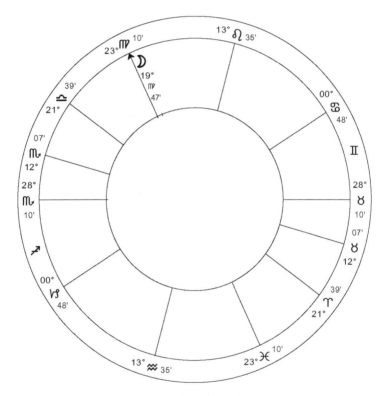

First Vaccination Chart

The Moon is the mother who cares for her children, and the sign of Virgo is one of service and healing. She was in the most visible and public place she could have been. It was an extraordinary omen: this vaccination programme was going to heal the world.

Six weeks later, the EU ran into problems when it did not receive the vaccine deliveries it had been hoping for, and this situation continued for some months afterwards. The EU has its own chart. There is a technique called Progression, where you can see the phases of life that an individual, or a country, is living through. And what do we find overhead? The Moon in Virgo. An identical signature to the vaccination chart.

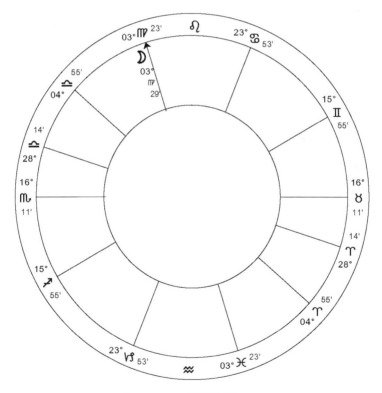

Progressed EU Chart

A Progressed Chart does not describe a moment of beginning, but a phase that lasts. Nevertheless, it shows clearly the concern of the EU to take care of and heal its peoples.

The astrological symbolism is remarkable, and that fact that it happened twice is even more so. It is enough to suspect a conspiracy by the gods!

Astrology doesn't just help us understand ourselves and events by revealing, through its symbols, factors of importance, and the connections between them. It also shows that the universe knows us, and that is a moment of enchantment that is ever fresh. I have been doing astrology readings, and writing about it, for many years. And still, when I see a signature like that Moon in Virgo, it takes my breath away.

Astrology enchants the universe in an age when that enchantment has been replaced by the notion of a dead universe, that the universe is just a thing and we are just one more thing in it. We are the first people in history to entirely forget our roots in spirit, in the sense that consciousness is fundamental.

Astrology doesn't just assert the enchanted nature of the universe: it demonstrates it over and over. In 'mundane' astrology – the astrology of worldly events – we often see this weird literalism in the correspondence between sky events and events on the ground. When I do a reading for someone, I begin by asking them to tell me as little as possible about themselves until I have talked about the chart for a while. On the one hand that keeps me more open to simply reading the symbols without pre-judgement, but it also gives the 'client' (as we call them nowadays) the experience of things being said about themselves and their history that are true and specific, and for them that is a moment of enchantment. It's like how could this guy possibly know these things? Well, it's not actually me that knows these things, it is all in the symbolism and the way I am prompted by who-knows-what to give a particular interpretation of those symbols.

Astrology has become quite mathematical in the last 2000 years, but originally it was based on what could be observed to be happening in the sky, in quite a simple way. What came to be the traditional meanings of sky events would have arisen through a combination of observation and inspiration, the same kind of prompt that you get in readings to interpret in a particular way. Several thousand years ago, Mars and Jupiter coming together in the sky could have meant that the Prince (Jupiter) would go to War (Mars). Quite simple and literal and, once the movements of the planets were understood, predictable well in advance.

There is a raw power to this type of astrology, because it is so simple, and because it can be observed, that is hard to achieve when you are dealing with bits of paper covered with numbers and arcane squiggles. That said, there is often nuance available from complexity, that is not so obvious when the symbolism is simple.

Sky events are not always observable. For example, if two planets are opposite, then one can be seen, but the other one is the other side of the earth, and cannot be seen. But there can still be that raw literalism that has its own kind of power.

A good example was 9/11, when two airliners, hijacked by al Qaeda operatives, were flown into the World Trade Centre. At that time, Saturn in Gemini was opposite Pluto in Sagittarius. Pluto can symbolise terror, and Sagittarius stands for that which that which is foreign, or for religious fundamentalism. Saturn symbolises hard work and achievement, and Gemini is of course the twins, just as the towers were twins. The symbolism here is eerily literal. But why did it happen in the USA?

For that we need to look at the chart for the US, created at its moment of inception, the Declaration of Independence on 4th July 1776. The 'correct' chart is debated, but the one that had achieved the most prominence was one that had the signs of Sagittarius and Gemini running along the East-West axis i.e., the constellation Sagittarius was on the Eastern horizon at the moment America was 'born', it is the Ascendant of the chart. Each of these constellations has 30 degrees, and the degrees of Saturn and Pluto at the time of 9/11 were close to the degrees of the US Ascendant.

US Chart and 9/11

So, running along the middle of the US chart at the moment of 9/11 were Saturn and Pluto in Gemini and Sagittarius, with a symbolism that was eerily apposite for the occasion. Ghastly as it was, the gods had their role in this event.

Everything, if you like, is dreamed into being from some bigger dimension than this one. And it is not about some happy 'evolution', which is just a recent human idea. It is not for us mere humans to pronounce on the designs of the gods, even though we may occasionally catch glimpses.

When we intend something and act, it sends ripples throughout the web of existence, because everything is connected. This material reality is not primary. Consciousness is primary, as quantum physics showed over 100 years ago. It will never catch on, just as astrology will never catch on, because it is too subtle, and people want simple certainties, so that they know where they stand.

For early peoples throughout the world, this material reality is dreamed into being. The world can seem absolutely real to us, it can seem like all there is. This is perhaps particularly so when we are young, when maybe it needs to appear like this, as we attempt to incarnate ourselves. But as death moves closer, our perspective changes, our convulsive identification with our bodily existence begins to loosen, and the dream-like nature of existence presents itself more strongly. And esoteric subjects like astrology start to make more sense. Not that it didn't always make sense for me: astrology had me gripped as a teenager.

But as my sense of the interconnected, dream-like nature of existence has slowly grown, so too do I feel more confident in the truths of astrology, and less inclined to try and 'prove' it scientifically.

Because reality is an interconnected dream, a significant event like the first vaccine will have reflections of itself in the cosmic weave, that can be read by those who know how, just as an Amazonian Brujo can read guinea-pig entrails.

OK, I admit it, I don't know how astrology works, and I never will, and I never want to. There are explanations to be had, as I started giving above and will return to and expand upon later. But really it is a mystery. Why should the Moon – the mother – appear in the sign of healing at the moment the first vaccine is given? There is no reason at all that this should happen. And that is precisely why astrology gives us this sense of wonder and awe, why it enchants the universe. It shows some other, magical order at work. Or should I say disorder. I will sometimes refer to it as the gods, sometimes as the Otherworld, sometimes as the web of existence. It doesn't matter. It is all that sense of something numinous and other and bigger than our tiny individual consciousnesses – the vast consciousness within which we have our existence. It is all these things, whatever it is that gives us this sense. When that bigger design shows itself, and it is usually fleeting, and cannot be pinned down, then we feel we are in the presence of something sacred, that has the highest value, that fills life with significance and meaning. And in which humour is also often present, in case this is all sounding a bit religious.

And this is a particular astrologer's particular view of the subject. When I was born, the Moon was in Sagittarius. So, to feel cared for and nourished (Moon) I need a sense of faith in some bigger order of things (Sagittarius). I think this is true for everyone – Sagittarians love to generalise about other people! – but it is a particular focus for me.

Reading an astrology chart is always an act of faith, for there is no good rational reason why any of it should work. Why should the position of the planet Mercury in the sky at the moment you were born say something about how your mind works? Or Venus say something about what type of person you are attracted to, or attract towards you? There is no rational or material reason for these things. And that is the wonder of it.

The examples I have given so far have been from mundane astrology. The charts of well-known people also reveal such synchronicities. The Eastern horizon is where the Sun rises and begins the day. It is therefore the place of beginnings. Whatever constellation was on the Eastern horizon at the moment we were born was therefore how we first met life, and how we continue to meet life. It is therefore often the sign that we first notice about other people. It is the Ascendant, or Rising Sign, as we have already seen in the case of the US chart (the 'Sibly' chart, as that particular one is known.)

When Donald Trump was born, the constellation Leo was on the Eastern horizon. Leo the lion is the king of the beasts, and in the same way Donald Trump has always felt himself to be special and kingly, and needed those around him to see him that way. I am not criticising him when I say this, just observing it. Good things can come out of this kind of temperament. It is not the place of astrology to make judgements, but rather to observe. Sometimes we think we are observing when in fact we are making judgements, and I will say more about this in Chapter 3. It is very difficult not to be judgemental, it is wired into us, but astrology requires us to be impeccable in this regard.

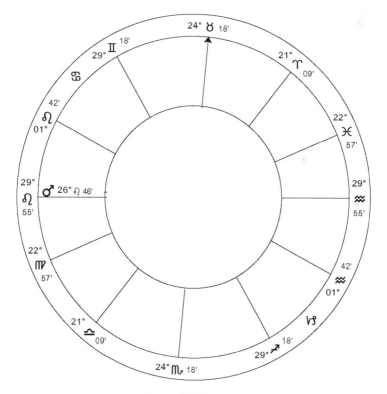

Donald Trump

Not only does Donald Trump have Leo Rising, but if you had looked at that place in the sky as he was born, you would also have seen the presence of the red planet Mars, God of war. (Note Mars and the Rising Sign are on the west of the chart rather than the east: it is one of the quirks of astrology charts that they invert these directions.) Mars – combativeness – is also basic to the way Donald Trump expresses himself. We all got to know this quality through the more than 25000 tweets he published during his Presidency. Life is a battle to be fought against enemies. This battle and its winning is so central to who he is, that he could not accept that he lost the 2020 Presidential election.

For me, when I see simple astrology working so strongly, as it does in the case of Trump, it gives me this sense of wonder and awe. The workings of the chart are not usually so obvious in the case of most people. Do they have a particular quality, or is it really something slightly different? When a planet is on the Rising Sign, however, it usually expresses itself particularly strongly, and when you combine that with an extreme character like Trump, you see the hand of the gods.

This is why astrology is not about good and bad. It certainly does not take the side of Democrats over Republicans, though watching the interpretations of some astrologers, you might be led to think so. Astrology is showing us the workings of the gods in everything, and therefore also revealing significances we might not otherwise have seen.

I will be mainly referring to this sense of something other as 'the gods' from now on, because that is consistent with the astrological paradigm, whereby the planets all have names of Greek and Roman gods, because they *are* those gods. They are not just lumps of rock. We will explore this idea more fully later on. If you are an astrologer, an ongoing contemplation of the nature of reality is natural, because there is no obvious mechanism or reason for these 'lumps of rock' to describe our lives, and yet they do.

Here is another piece of literal astrology that continues to gobsmack me. Neil Armstrong, the first man on the Moon, was born with the Moon at 25 degrees and 23 minutes of Sagittarius. At that time, the Galactic Centre was at 25 degrees and 53 minutes of Sagittarius. So, the Moon was exactly aligned with the centre of our galaxy at the moment he was born. Armstrong had an appointment with Destiny written in the stars.

This does, of course, raise issues of Fate and Free Will. I think both have their place. They are only contradictory from a narrow point of view. (See Chapter 13.)

The two strongest points in the sky are the Eastern horizon (where the Sun rises and begins the day), and the overhead point (where the Sun is at its strongest). That is why in the examples I have used planets that are overhead (the MC) or on the Ascendant. It is fairly obvious why a planet overhead should be expressing itself strongly, but in the case of a rising planet, it is strong because astrology is about beginnings. The basic idea of astrology is that the beginning of a life contains the blueprint for its whole future unfoldment, like the seed of a tree. And because everything is interconnected, that future unfoldment can be read in the configuration of the universe at the moment of inception.

Chapter 2

Keeping it Simple

I like to keep astrology simple, because it is then easier to remain close to the symbolism. When you are close to the symbolism, when you feel it strongly, it can speak through you. Anyone can learn the set of meanings of the planets and signs and put them together to read a chart. A computer can do that. But that is not astrology, because it is not the gods speaking through you, but the intellect, which needs to be the servant, not the master.

When I am doing readings, I concentrate on the Sun and Moon and Rising Sign, and draw everything else in around them. You can do a perfectly good reading with just the Sun and the Moon and nothing else. The reason for this is that we already have a strong experiential relationship with them, because they are by far the two biggest objects in the sky. We see the Sun and Moon whether we like it or not, we see them change and move. Our unconscious already has a powerful relationship with them that is hundreds of thousands of years old. Our ancestors had the sense to make offerings and express gratitude to the Sun for making life possible. Some of them had the idea that if we did not express our appreciation to the Sun every day, it would stop rising and the world would come to an end. That idea may not make much sense to our rational, scientific minds. But it makes complete sense to our unconscious minds. The unconscious takes such ideas literally, and I don't think we shall go far wrong if we do too.

When you have a strong relationship with a planet – a god, because it is a living thing – then it can speak through you. The Sun and the Moon in a chart can speak through anyone, because we all have a strong relationship with them.

So let us look at a simplified chart in this way. Charts of

famous people are very useful in this way, because most of us know them. Political figures are tricky, because most of us are very biased all the time either for or against them (without actually knowing them very well), but maybe on a good day some of us are only a bit biased. Let us begin by being honest about that, otherwise astrology is not possible. Celebrities tend to be culture specific, whereas most people know, for example, the US Presidents.

Below is a simplified Sun-Moon chart for Barack Obama.

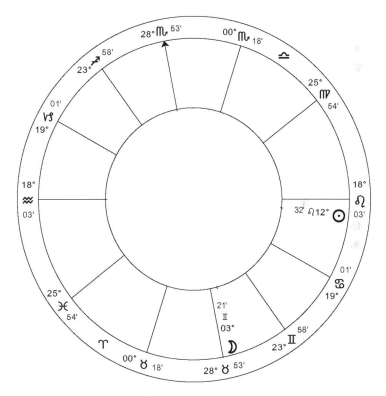

Barack Obama

A chart such as this shows you the main things you need to know about someone. Let us begin with a physical sense of the Sun and the Moon at the moment Obama was born. It was early evening. The Sun had set just 20 minutes earlier, so there was still a glow on the western horizon, with the Sun hanging weightily just below it. Meanwhile, almost directly below our feet, on the other side of the earth, was that other weighty object, the Moon, usually about the same size as the Sun, and sometimes, when near the horizon, bigger. This is to talk experientially, rather than scientifically, and let us not be too quick to dismiss our sense experience as 'false': what else do we have, in the last analysis, than our experience? Mother nature gives the male and female, Sun and Moon, equal weight, but sometimes makes the female, the foundation of life, bigger, as if to remind us.

Astronomers tell us that the masculine is far bigger than the feminine, the Sun far bigger than the Moon, but their method is based on a rational, male way of thinking, so they would, wouldn't they? Thinking mythologically is just as necessary, and just as real, as thinking literally, and this is a theme to which we shall return. Astrology definitely prioritises mythological thinking.

Anyway, we can get an almost physical sense of these two planets hanging there in the sky in their respective positions, the Father and the Mother. This sort of exercise can be like a ritual beginning to the reading. It invokes the unconscious, it pleases the gods, and they will respond by speaking through us.

Divination – which is the kind of knowledge that astrology is, rather than scientific – involves a transmission from spirit to matter. So being physically present to ourselves, and having a sense of the sky as a physical presence – rather than squiggles on paper – increases the oracular power of the astrologer.

First of all, Obama's Sun and Moon are below the horizon. So, he has an introverted temperament. Even though he was very public for a while, he is quite professorial, thoughtful, even bookish (he gives us lists of books he has been reading – what other ex-President does that?) Sure, he can turn on the Leo and be very appealing to people, he can strongly project who he is.

But it is not his everyday personality. The Moon in Gemini

– his emotional nature – is in the private, home – and family – loving 4th House. His family occupied a large place in our awareness of him. At the same time, this placement is good at articulating (Gemini) emotion (Moon). And that is his genius (Leo): this guy, seemingly coming from nowhere, electrifying the crowds (just as Trump did, from the other end of the political spectrum, also apparently from nowhere, eight years later. He too has a Leo-Gemini combination, in his case Ascendant and Moon.)

With the Sun in the 6th, Obama is motivated by a sense of service. With Aquarius Rising, in a dynamic opposition to his Sun, he broke the mould by becoming the first black President, and then bringing in substantial reform in healthcare, a 6th house concern, which Democrat Presidents had been struggling, and failing, to do for decades.

Already we have the main lineaments of who Obama is. We can take it further by looking at the elements: the Sun is in a fire sign (Leo) and an Earth house (the 6th). The Moon is in an air sign (Gemini) and in a watery house (4th). The Rising Sign is in air.

The elements are more basic than the signs. You can say a lot about someone by just looking at the elements. When I do readings, I often get half way through before I remember to look at them, because I get entranced by the planets.

However, I do not regard that as a failing. Some astrologers do good readings in a systematic way. That is not my way. I see astrology as (hopefully) the gods speaking through me, and that works best for me if I begin the reading by what first attracts my attention. I make a point of trusting that. If I get my rational mind, with its desire to systematise, out of the way then other things can happen. Everything does eventually get covered, but in its own order.

So, each planet has an element by sign, and an element by house. There is a correspondence between the houses and the signs, so you can work out the element of a house by its number:

the 6th house corresponds to the 6th sign, which is Virgo, which is Earth.

The basic difference between the sign of a planet and its house is that the sign emphasises its inner aspect, its essential character, and the house emphasises the way it acts in the world, or is obliged to act. The Rising Sign governs the 1st house, so the basic way we are 'obliged' to act is according to the nature of that sign. It is not a part of us, in the way that a planet is. It is a doorway through which we are continually stepping. And that may be easy or difficult, depending on the rest of our chart.

Barack Obama has an airy Ascendant (Aquarius) and that flows well with both his airy Moon and fiery Sun: his Ascendant, with its Aquarian bent, is a lens through which he can easily also be his Sun and Moon. And that is even better for a Leo, because they are the Sign above all that has to be who they are.

The air and fire signs find it easy to understand each other, as do earth and water. Air and fire are both moving elements, whereas earth and water are more static, containing elements, masculine and feminine respectively. It is when we combine across these pairings that we are challenged. They are growth points.

So, Barack Obama is challenged in this way in both his Sun and Moon. Life requires him to incarnate in ways that do not come easily to him. And this challenge is fundamental, because it involves both his Sun and Moon, the main part of who he is. For his Sun, it is a matter of 'Don't tell me about your visions unless they grow corn'. His visionary Sun in Leo can only fulfil itself through everyday activity, through work and service. He cannot be the *puer aeternus* who avoids getting his hands dirty in the 'mundane' world. Getting his healthcare bill through congress was a good example of the synergy between these two contrasting elements.

It is tempting to idealise Obama, just as it is tempting to demonise Donald Trump. We can use the discipline of astrology to train ourselves out of those unconscious – and natural – ways of being. We can begin by not ignoring facts. For Obama, Tuesdays became his killing day, the day he signed off on all the assassinations that would be carried out by drone that week in the Middle East. Indeed, it was under Obama that drone assassinations began. For him, it became a regular, everyday, 6th house matter. To be a political leader, you need this shadow side, and it probably needs to be compartmentalised and not fully acknowledged in your psyche. Drones, and the distance they create from human realities, facilitate this process. As does the description of those you are killing as enemies.

There is another characterisation of the signs, into cardinal, fixed and mutable or, in the case of the houses, angular, succedent and cadent. They have much the same meanings in both signs and houses, in terms of initiating, establishing and adapting. Obama's Sun is fixed fire, it shines steadily, one of his beaming grins was never far away, and his vision sustained itself. His Sun also found itself in cadent Earth: it had to be adaptable, easy-going as well as practical. And this was again good for dealing with Congress: you have to be endlessly adaptable and flexible to get any laws through them. And in a darker way, he could be easy-going about signing off on the weekly assassinations.

So, Obama's Sun is challenged not just by the contrast between the elements of its sign and house, but also by 'quadruplicity'. These challenges make for a creative personality, if we are willing to rise to them, and the astrology does not tell us that. Astrology tells us what type of person we are, and the choices we have, but not the choices we will make. There is something central and essential to us that only we know ourselves.

Obama's Moon is in an air sign, and a watery (4th) house. The air is in mutable Gemini, the Water in the Angular 4th. I am deliberately piling all this complexity into one sentence to make the point that there is a lot that can be said about someone just by going into detail about their Sun and Moon.

Astrology in this sense is like a Mandelbrot set. You can go into just one part of the chart, and then expand it into the whole by drawing out the detail. But in this case, we still have just these two big, powerful symbols in our minds, rather than a host of them, and that has its own divinatory power.

So, back to Obama's Moon. It is in an air sign and watery house. The Moon is a watery planet anyway (ruling Cancer), so it is comfortable in the 4th house. The combination of these two means that Obama cannot be emotionally at ease unless he is articulating and communicating (Gemini) what he feels (Moon) in a way that initiates change (angular) in his family/tribe (4th House). And this is indeed what he did in his campaigning for Presidency: his slogan of "Yes we can" was a message of hope. The adaptable, easy-going mutable Moon was challenged by the angular House it was in to set others on fire. The facility with words of his airy Moon was challenged by the watery 4th House to find words for real emotion. A clear example was his grief at the school shootings, where he wept in public and implored Congress to think again about gun laws.

Gemini is the sign of the light twin and the dark twin. Their challenge is to get to know and to make friends with each other. We have already noted the drone assassinations. There was also the killing of Osama bin Laden, which delighted Obama, and he had no hesitation in expressing that. As a political leader, these actions may sometimes be necessary. But they are solemn, they are not there to be delighted in. The name of the operation, 'Geronimo', likened the hunting down of bin Laden to that of a troublesome Native American. If Obama was a true African-American (he wasn't: his father was Kenyan) he would have understood the minority oppression in the US and called the operation something else.

Obama's Moon in Gemini describes well his emotional compartmentalisation, which is maybe necessary, as already stated, in a politician, but it maybe something he will be able to address as he moves into being an elder statesman. I was quite shocked early in Obama's campaign to be President, when he abruptly disowned his erstwhile spiritual mentor, the Reverend Wright, who had been caught on video saying that 9/11 was America's chickens coming home to roost for its actions in the Middle East. That seemed a fair enough – even obvious – point to me. Rev Wright is black, and does not feel constrained by the same type of patriotism that the whites feel, for his community has been on the sharp end of white American imperialism. It is not a viable position, however, for a politician, and so Obama disowned Wright. And it seemed to me that he meant it. Obama could only see America in relation to the rest of the world through white American eyes. This was for real, and it had to be, or he would not have been elected.

The 4ᵗʰ house also describes the early family background. Its twin Geminian nature reflects his American mother and Kenyan father.

We can also draw in the signs on the cusps of the houses in which we find his Sun and Moon – Cancer and Taurus respectively. One point here is that the Moon is the ruler of Cancer, Obama's 6ᵗʰ house cusp, in which we find his Sun. And that brings a connection to his Sun and Moon, it means his Sun can be an expression of his Moon, the visionary Leo and the emotionally articulate Gemini can function as one.

I think enough has been said to make the point that astrology can be kept very simple and therefore close to the symbolism and the divinatory power that comes with it; and yet a lot can be drawn out of that easily enough, on the Mandelbrot principle, for a substantial reading, in which the astrologer has to decide what to leave out.

However, I also want to take a look at Obama's progressed Sun and Moon, just to complete the picture, because they say something about the phases of life that an individual is passing through.

Astrology works through symbolic correspondences. For example, the planet Mars is also the god Mars and is also the principle of assertion in the human psyche. Progressions work on the principle that one rotation of Earth on its own axis corresponds to one circuit of Earth around the Sun. Days, in other words, correspond to years. The 10th day of your life says something about the 10th year of your life.

The progressed Sun and Moon move relatively quickly, and so can describe much of the changes that occur as we move through life. The progressed Sun moves a degree every year, the progressed Moon moves a degree every month, whereas the progressed outer planets hardly move at all during the course of a lifetime, so are not very significant, because it is movement that creates change. That is why the Moon is the activator of the whole chart in medieval astrology, because she moves the fastest. And the same in the progressed chart.

Barack Obama's natal Sun is at 12 Leo. In 2008, the year he was first elected President, his progressed Moon opposed his natal Sun from 12 Aquarius, and then went on to cross his natal Ascendant at 18 Aquarius just before his inauguration in January 2009. His Leo Sun was being dynamically activated, it was coming into a new fullness as he campaigned to be President. And it was happening from radical, rule-breaking, humanitarian Aquarius, all those things that Obama stood for. This new departure that he stood for was confirmed by the progressed Moon subsequently crossing his natal Ascendant.

A couple of years into his Presidency, his progressed Sun changed sign from Virgo to Libra. A Progressed planet changing sign is always significant, because it happens rarely. In the case of the Sun, it happens once every 30 years, and there is a lead-in to it for a few years. Your natal Sun remains the same, but you are having an experience of, learning that new sign. Obama remained a Leo – and with his easy assumption of kingship, he is a classic Leo – but was moving, as he became President, into an experience of Libra: the need to work in partnership, to negotiate, if you are going to get any laws passed.

There is also the progressed Sun-Moon cycle. We can look at the aspects the prog (progressed) planets are making to the natal chart, as we did with Obama's prog Moon and natal Sun. But the prog planets also make aspects among themselves, and the most important prog cycle is that between the Sun and the Moon, which takes about 30 years.

When they come together, it is like the planting of a new seed, a new paradigm. It takes the first quarter of the cycle, about seven years, to start to see clearly what it is. And then 15 years in, it reaches the maximum, when the prog Moon is opposite the prog Sun. It is a time when our life is abundant, it is at a peak. This occurred for Obama towards the end of his first term as President, and just before he was about to start campaigning successfully for a second term. This cycle began in 1997, when he was first elected as a Senator: he had a prog New Moon in Virgo in the prog 6th house. So, he began his political career in a spirit of service, by progressed sign (Virgo) and house (6th).

This progressed chart for Obama works really well. I knew his natal chart well before I started writing about it here, but I did not know his progressed chart: I did not choose it because it worked well. When someone's life has a clear outer trajectory, as Obama's does, seeing the correspondences between their life and the astrology can be fairly straightforward. Most of our lives are probably not so clearly demarcated in an outward way, and many of the progressed aspects will probably correspond as much to inner events as to outer events.

Astrologers are much more than fortune-tellers these days. We use the chart to describe the inner lives of ourselves and our clients, which is often our abiding interest. But you can't put your finger on inner events so clearly. Politicians tend not to have so much of this kind of inner awareness. They can happily on the one hand sign off on drone assassinations on a regular basis, and on the other hand improve the nation's healthcare and weep over school shootings. They are primarily interested in bringing change through outer events, and that can be hard to do if you are forever being scrupulous about your motives.

I'll bring in my own chart here. First of all, my natal chart.

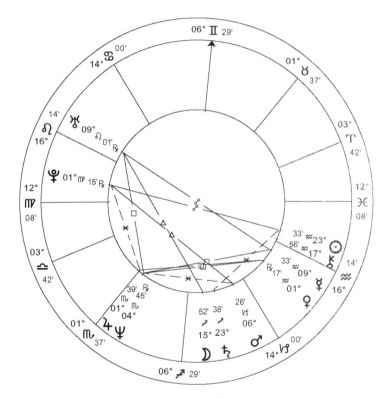

Author's Chart

And now my progressed chart from 1993, when I had a progressed New Moon in Pisces. That cycle is due to end in 2023.

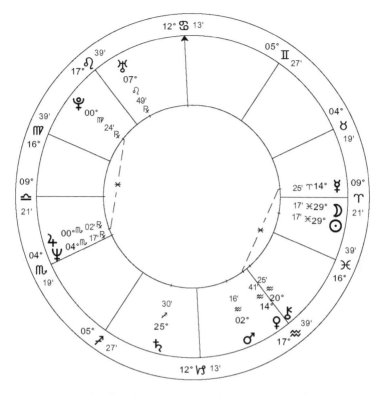

Author's Progressed Chart 1993

When I had that prog New Moon, I was 35 and in a state of semi-paralysis with my life, because my previous very wilful way of going about things no longer worked. I was slowly learning to surrender to a deeper spirit in myself, to the gods if you like, instead of thinking I could plan it all and do it all myself. And that theme, which is also one of trust, is very Piscean, and it has been a long, slow learning process. At the time of writing (2021) I am in the run-up to the next prog New Moon in 2023, which will be in Aries, and here I am writing my first book on astrology. Aries likes to do things early; it likes to just get on with it. A few weeks before the prog Moon moved into Aries, I began writing my first book, which was on the Medicine Wheel, followed rapidly by this book.

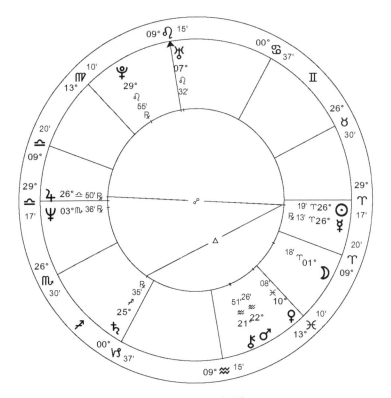

Author's Progressed Chart 2021

So, after all these years of Piscean surrender to the Spirit, of learning to be imbued with Spirit instead of my own wilfulness, it is as if I am being told OK, you are ready to do something with it now, off you go. But this long process is probably not something that is obvious from the outside, unlike the way in which the shifts in Obama's life can be clearly seen.

These first two chapters have each, in their own way, emphasised the power of simple astrology. In the first chapter, it was the power of planets on Angles, where they traditionally manifest most strongly. In the second chapter, it was the divinatory power that comes from being close to the symbols, feeling them as an almost physical presence, and using the two planets that are the strongest in this sense, the Sun and the Moon.

This simple approach may also manifest in other ways. A

planet may just leap out at you in a chart, and you don't know why. Trust it when that happens. Astrology is fundamentally divinatory rather than scientific and systematic.

If you've been in an astrology group, you may have noticed that if someone brings in a theme via a planet and maybe an aspect to it, other people quickly contribute by bringing in complexity – other aspects the planet is making, what the house cusp ruler is doing, what the transits are, the Sabian symbol for that degree, or maybe there are one or two asteroids nearby.

That complexity does give us more information, I do not want to put it down in any way, because it is central to astrology. Indeed, one of the signs of a good astrologer is the ability to synthesise the complexity and make something telling of it.

However, by quickly moving on to complexity from the fact that, say Venus is in Pisces in that person's chart, by not letting it just hang there and feeling it, we lose something important. When a symbol is just sitting there in our being, it has a lot of power.

Astrology needs to be slow so that the symbols can be felt. This is often difficult in groups, where everyone wants to say their bit, often by adding complexity, and it can become very 'heady' and technique oriented. A typical event at an astrology group may be a talk about a new technique someone has found. And that can be exciting, because it may tell us things we had not thought of before. But really, we don't need new techniques, if anything we need less of them.

The Buddhist tradition sometimes talks about 'higher teachings', and that keeps people interested. Of course, we all want a 'higher teaching', because we've maybe got a bit bored with the 'lower teachings'. But there is no such thing as a 'higher teaching'. What could be more profound than Buddhism's basic teaching of impermanence, for example?

I think it is a bit like that in astrology, with the abundance of techniques, as well as asteroids that we can add into the chart. They all seem to add in these extra nuggets of meaning and interest. And they do. But as I hope I showed in my discussion of Obama's Sun and Moon, we can draw out probably everything we need from the basics. They are only lacking if we are not feeling them, and if we are not feeling them, then that severely limits our divinatory abilities.

When you read a chart, there are any number of places you can go to with it. I think it is best to allow one or two planets (or asteroids, if you use them) to come forward, and then prioritise them, sit with them and that will allow the gods or goddesses behind those planets to speak.

There is often something central that is wanting to come out in the reading, and that needs space. It is remarkable how often I think I am coming to the end of a reading, everything has been covered, and then suddenly out something leaps that turns out to be the main point of the reading, the real reason the person is there (which may be quite different to what they thought), and so I find myself in conversation for another half hour. I try to keep readings open-ended for that reason. If it wants to go on for two hours (and these things are not under my control) then I trust that and go with it. If not a lot seems to be happening in a reading, somehow you don't seem to be getting to the heart of anything, trust that too. It is not about us, the astrologer. It is about the gods speaking, or not speaking (apparently, sometimes.) We just need to do our craft while, in a bigger sense, staying out of the way.

All that said, I see astrology as a divinatory art for people with active left brains. It is as though our minds can need the complexity to keep them busy and out of the way so that we can get on with being intuitive. And some of the best astrology can come from synthesis of complex patterns, as if one throws that pattern into the unconscious and see what emerges. I don't want to be prescriptive. But however, we do our astrology, I think space needs to be left to feel the symbolism and patterns, allow them to drift around a bit inside us.

Chapter 3

Prediction, Political Astrology and Bad Astrology

In 2016, shortly before the US Presidential election, a panel of 12 reputable astrologers was asked at an astrology conference in the US to predict who would win the election, Donald Trump or Hillary Clinton. Eleven of them predicted that Hillary Clinton would win.

I found this fascinating. It highlighted a number of issues: most obviously, the alleged liberal bias in the astrological community, which has been commented on for years; the need for disinterest to do astrology properly; and the matter of predictability itself.

I don't have a list of who the astrologers were, so there is nothing personal in it. I am not saying they were all showing bias, nor am I saying that the astrologer who correctly predicted Trump did not do so for reasons of bias also! It is hard to say in any individual case. But when 11 out of 12 get it wrong, it is hard to avoid the conclusion that some of these astrologers were predicting the outcome that they wanted.

You can use astrology to justify just about anything. Here is an example, the Solar Return chart for the USA for 2001, the year of the 9/11 attacks. The Solar Return is a chart for the year, based on the Sun being in the position it was in when the country – or the person – was born, which occurs once a year.

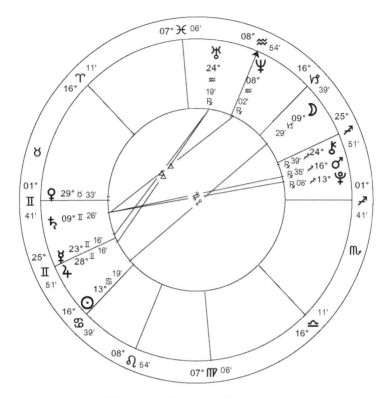

US Solar Return Chart 2001

I wrote a blog in 2008, using this chart to make the case that 9/11 was not a government set-up. I said that the Mars-Pluto conjunction in Sagittarius in the 7th House showed an attack by foreign terrorists, and Neptune on the Midheaven showed that the government had been caught napping. 'No', said someone who firmly believed that 9/11 was a government conspiracy: Neptune on the Midheaven shows that it was a government deception, and Mars-Pluto in Sag in the 7th indicates the presence of a controlling foreign partner. 'Like who', I said, who on earth controls the US to that extent? 'Israel', she suggested. Well yes, the hold of the Israeli lobby over who even gets as far as being a candidate for Congress has been documented. But attacking the World Trade Center and the Pentagon with airliners, using Arabs as cover? Come on.

I think I had facts and reason and plausibility on my side, but that is usually beside the point in these sorts of cases where strong beliefs are at stake. You can see how we both used the astrology to justify our own beliefs about 9/11. And how some at least of that panel of astrologers in 2016 used whatever method they were using (and they each had their own method) to come to the conclusion that Hilary Clinton, their preferred candidate, would win the election.

The kind of disinterest needed to do good political or mundane astrology is rare, even amongst astrologers with good reputations, who have been at it for decades. Particularly when it comes to politics, it can be hard for people to see that their view is just a view, and not reality itself. I was once debating on Facebook with a friend, and I was arguing for the view of a particular US politician, and her response was 'But he's a Republican!' as though that ended the argument. The moral psychologist Jonathan Haidt says something similar about himself. He said that when he first went to university in the US, he and his friends were all Democrats, and they sincerely assumed that anyone who voted Republican had something wrong with them, something bad must have happened to them in their childhood to explain it.

There is nothing wrong with having leanings one way or the other in politics, but I don't think we have a hope of doing decent political astrology if we have such a dismissive attitude towards people who don't vote our way, like they have something wrong with them.

If you can appreciate the values of the parties you don't vote for, if you can appreciate the fact that the other half of the population has values that are genuine, that just aren't the same as yours, then you are in with a chance of doing some useful political astrology. Otherwise, forget it!

Jonathan Haidt refers to this as the 'Moral Matrix' that so many people are caught in. It seems to be liberals he particularly wants to address, probably because they tend to be more open-minded than conservatives. You can easily look up his TED talk on 'The Moral Roots of Conservatives and Liberals', and I urge you to watch it before you read any further.

As a moral psychologist, he has done a lot of research into the different values held by Liberals and Conservatives. This left-right split is worldwide. People on the left tend to prioritise caring for people. People on the right have what he calls the 'insight' that order and stability are hard-won and easily lost. They also value caring for people, but they place it on a par with order and stability, rather than prioritising it in the way the left does.

There are other values as well, but these are the main two, and they seem quite commonsensical, like something we already knew about the left and the right. But the point is to appreciate that the values held by the other side are genuine and something we can value also. The left are not just bleeding-heart liberals who will wreck the economy; and the right are not just selfish bastards who only care about the rich and privileged.

When Haidt says 'The Moral Matrix', he means it in the sense of the film, *The Matrix*, in which people are trapped within an illusory world without realising it, and they are offered the blue pill or the red pill: with the blue pill they can carry on as before, comfortable in their illusions and with no need for the stress and anxiety of change; the red pill, on the other hand, reveals the world-as-it-is, and is that something we really want? As TS Eliot said,

"Humankind cannot bear very much reality"

In this case, the world-as-it-is reveals that our political opponents also have something we need to listen to, they are genuine, and do we want to go there? This is something very difficult for most people to do, but as I say, without this shift, political astrology is not possible. Rather, we end up misusing astrology to justify our own prejudices.

It is human nature to be one-sided on just about everything, and out of that we create an identity, defined as much by what we are against as what we are for. If you can step out of that matrix with politics, I think you can do it just about anywhere, because it is such a big one.

As an astrologer or therapist or any sort of healer, this kind of disinterest is basic to what we do. It's called self-awareness, in the sense of the ability to stand back from our immediate experience and assumptions, and weigh a situation according to facts and reason. It is the quality of air (mind) at its best, unlike the usual misuse of air, which is to use it to put a layer of reason on emotionally-based beliefs and preferences.

I know very few astrologers who can treat someone like Donald Trump with the necessary disinterest. It can almost seem sometimes like they feel it is their job to use astrology to confirm what a bad guy he is. But as has often been said, you could not have predicted Hitler from his chart. There is something at the centre of who we are, maybe the most important part, that the chart does not reveal. The gods may choose to reveal it to you if you are an intuitive astrologer, but the chart alone doesn't.

It is not our job to make moral judgements about people. When we make judgements, there is usually something in it for us, and that is when it slides over into being 'judgemental': we get a sense of satisfaction from putting the other person down, because it puts us, fragile creatures that we are, up.

Donald Trump is a very interesting exercise from this point of view. My personal opinion is that he was not fit to be President of the USA, but I am saying that as a way of owning that view, so that I can (hopefully) then do some astrology. The tendency of us humans to project our shadow sides onto politicians is very strong. We need the ones from the other side to be the bad guys, and that can seem to us simply to be reality. Hence the Moral Matrix. And for this reason, it can be hard to get a word of sense from people about Trump. He is such a good bad guy!

If you are going to look at a politician, you need to put aside how you feel about them, and the judgements that come from that, and look at things like what they have said they want to do, and whether they tried to do it. It never occurs to a lot of people that someone like Trump would have any policies among the nearly incomprehensible things he used to regularly come out with. To allow him to have any actual policies seems too much, it is taking him more seriously than he deserves. But that is just us responding with nonsense to his nonsense.

Trump had certain enduring convictions, and that is what got him elected. The electorate may be uninformed and prejudiced, but people can usually tell if someone is for real, and if they are not, if they don't themselves believe what they are saying, people can tell, and won't vote for them.

Trump had the simple convictions of a businessman. He believed, for example, that the trade with China had become very imbalanced, that China was engaged in many unfair trade practices, and he was determined to address that. He did indeed begin to address that, in his bar-room brawler style, which is his Mars on the Ascendant. He also thought the other NATO countries should pay their fair share towards its costs, and he tried to do something about that too.

These sort of things need looking at, as well as character traits like the narcissism with which his Leo Rising expressed itself. This narcissism was obvious to everyone, but it is not our place as astrologers to judge him for that, to call him 'a narcissist'. Nobody is 'a' anything, for that is to fix and damn them, using psychological terminology to do so. People are verbs, and they sometimes behave in certain ways.

We approach the collective shadow at our peril, because we will be damned for it, even in the astrological world. Trump was such a brilliant hook for the shadow, for our need to have someone to be the bad guy, so that if you said anything that wasn't damning of him, that tried to be objective, you would immediately become suspect in many people's eyes. Liberals engage in shadow projection, are just as unconscious in this respect, as anyone else. I remain a Trump supporter in some people's eyes simply because I tried to be objective about him.

If you want to do political astrology, you've got to be prepared to stick your neck out in this way, and ignore what other people think of you. You've got to be able to take the heat. It takes courage, it takes character, and I recommend it.

Here is another example. It was from an astrology group I attended, which decided to look at the chart of Boris Johnson. I couldn't do much more than sit there aghast. It began with an introduction to Johnson in which his character was described in a contemptuous way; with the school he went to being one of the reasons we should not think highly of him. This is something many of us do: we make character assessments of politicians on the basis of very little evidence, and almost certainly without having met them personally, in a way that we might feel outraged if we saw someone talking about someone we actually knew. In other words, those character assessments, and those assumptions of motive, are largely nonsense, they are prejudice, they are barely worth listening to.

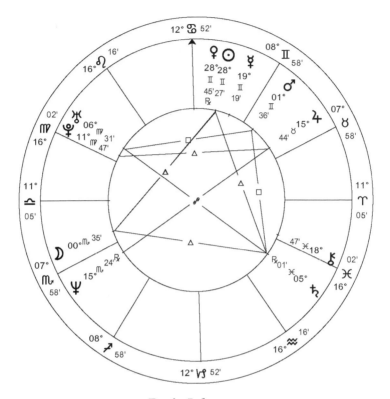

Boris Johnson

Having introduced Johnson in this way, the group began to look for the strong Neptune in his chart. He had to have a strong Neptune, because he is a deceptive character: this was assumed as a fact. As you can see from Johnson's chart, the only major aspect his Neptune makes is its opposition to Jupiter. His Neptune is probably less strong than in most charts. Undeterred, the group began to look at his harmonic charts and eventually, and probably inevitably, found one with a reasonably prominent Neptune. At that, the person who was the main advocate for Johnson's strong Neptune displayed a smug satisfaction. He had had an insight that Johnson has a strong Neptune, and he had eventually been proved right.

Where do you begin in addressing this kind of non-astrology? I chose not to begin, and I decided there was no point continuing to be part of such a group. What I reckoned that people were seeing – if they were seeing anything apart from their own prejudices – was the pronounced Gemini in his chart, which can be quite tricksy and as we know in Johnson's case, could be 'flexible' at best with the truth. One of the great things about a political astrology chart, properly used, is that it gives us a break from our own prejudices, it gives us a chance to be self-aware, if that is what we want. It is often not what people want. In this case, it would be a matter of saying that you felt Johnson to be a deceptive character, is that true, and if it is true, what type of deceptiveness is it? Clearly from the chart, it is a Geminian rather than a Neptunian deceptiveness. They are quite different, and an interesting and nuanced discussion can arise on that basis. Always, of course, backed up by facts, because maybe the perception of deceptiveness was partly just prejudice in the first place. In this way, astrology can be used to get to know a politician and to get to know ourselves. I think it is a kind of sorcery to use this magical art simply to confirm our own prejudices.

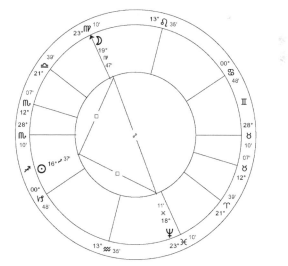

First Vaccination
In the chart for the first use of the Covid Vaccine, with which

I began this book, Neptune is opposite the Moon and square to the Sun. One experienced astrologer commented to me that this 'announced' deception, illusion and untruths. This is not something you can accurately say. Neptune can mean a lot of things. It may mean deception. Or it may mean, for example, redemption, which experience of the vaccine has borne out in a striking fashion. It may of course be both, but at the time of writing, no large-scale deception around the vaccine has been uncovered or even suggested. Any good astrologer would know that Neptune does not 'announce' deception, it merely indicates it as a possibility. What I reckon this comment was rooted in was the anti-establishment attitude that is so common in 'spiritual' and astrological circles, where it is taken almost as a fact that whatever the government says it is doing, it is in reality up to something else, and you are naïve if you do not get this.

That said, I don't think we need hard evidence to make suppositions based on astrology. That would be a one-sided earth attitude (see the Chapter 11 on the elemental balance). We may be using intuition (fire), which is by definition knowledge without any obvious evidence for it. This is a large part of astrology: the fact that we can tell people about themselves without knowing them enchants the universe for them, as well as getting them to pay attention to things we say about them that they may not, initially, agree with. It is a matter of being clear as to the source of what you are saying. In the case of the vaccine chart, if Neptune prompted you to say you think there will be a big deception around it, then say so. But don't insist on it, and be clear that Neptune does not have to mean this.

And even more important, be clear about your own pipework, that there isn't an exaggerated suspicion of the establishment informing your 'intuition' (which is very common). This is the 'hollow-bone' principle that you find amongst Native American healers. We need to get out of the way so that the

Spirit can speak through us in an unencumbered fashion. It is a life's work to be able to do this. And when you speak from your intuition, check it out afterwards. We probably learn more from the times we were wrong than when we were right. Be prepared to be wrong, we are bound to be some of the time, and there is no shame in it, even though some people may delight in our wrongness.

It is very common to find an unholy alliance of left-bias and anti-authority attitudes informing what passes for political astrology. Astrology as a technique is the easy part of becoming a competent astrologer. The hard part is those years of being honest with oneself, and stepping outside of group attitudes, that lend the necessary disinterestedness and objectivity to read a chart.

Astrologers are, in the popular imagination, able to read the future, and people may come to us to be told what is going to happen. What astrology teaches us, ironically, is just how unpredictable the future is. It is certainly possible to make some reasonably accurate predictions for people, at least in terms of the overall shape of their lives. It is much harder to be correct about specific events.

Astrology has swung sharply away from prediction in modern times, it has become a bit of a 'no-no'. I'm not sure why that is, but it seems a pity, because there can be a lot of value in it. It probably has to do with a desire to appear respectable, even scientific, which is a fool's errand, because astrology is not a science in the way the word is understood nowadays. Unable to help themselves, astrologers now talk about 'forecasting' instead, as though that is somehow not prediction! The point about divination is that it involves knowledge from some other source, it is 'out-there', it is magical, it has a deep appeal for people. It is why *Harry Potter* was so popular. And *Lord of the Rings*. People want magic. It needs be written in as a basic human right in the UN charter. Of course, people only want so much magic, they usually want to retreat to the safety of their well-defined lives afterwards. When you make a prediction, and it comes true, I think that changes people's relationship with the universe, it enchants it.

It can also be a bit tricky, however, because people can hang on to what you say as a substitute for their own self-knowing, whether that is to do with their basic character as revealed by the chart, or to do with predictions about the future. And whatever you say, some people will take any qualifications out of what you may have said. Our job is to use astrology to nudge people towards their own self-understanding, but they can so easily use astrology as a substitute for that.

One person came to me who had just got involved with a man 21 years her junior, and the reading concerned the future of the relationship. I began by asking "What is it you want me to say?" The premise of this reading, it seemed to me, was not so much about discerning the relationship for herself (it didn't last very long), but hoping that Fate would tell her that it was going to work out in the way she wanted.

The outer planets are the big transformers, and when they make challenging aspects to someone's birth chart, you can be sure there is big change coming up. Much of my work as an astrologer involves talking people through those often difficult periods, and showing them how the stars are holding their hand as they live through it.

I will use a politician as a simple illustration. Let's take someone from the political left, because so many people find it so hard to think straight if they are from the right. Below is Bill Clinton's chart, with the transits for Jan 20 1993 on the outside.

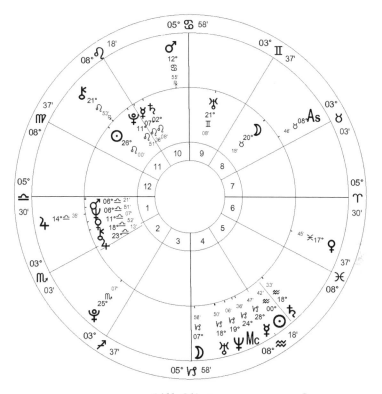

Bill Clinton

If he had come to me for a reading in the late 1980s, I would have said to him that he had a major empowerment of his life coming up in the early 90s as Pluto in Scorpio squared his Leo Sun. I would also have said that he would have to fight for that empowerment, he would have to claim it, and that it would expose some of his shadow material. I wouldn't have known what that empowerment would be, just that it would be happening. And of course, he became President of the USA in early 1993. If he had elaborated and told me he would be running for President, I would have said, well, it's going to be a very big deal for you one way or the other, even if you don't become the candidate, it will change who you are in a big way. Something that is new will be born in you. As for the shadow material, Clinton became known as the 'come-back kid' during his campaign, because unsavoury allegations around

41

women kept surfacing. His approach was one of denial, which is what politicians do, and he kept getting away with it. (With Venus-Neptune on his Libra Ascendant, he had all the charisma he needed to get away with just about anything.) In a sense, they have to deny it all, certainly if they want to get elected. But it means the shadow material, as described by the Pluto transit, doesn't get faced in the way that it might do in the case of an individual trying to become more aware.

This sort of prediction is very basic, and I think it is part of our job, it is a responsibility that we have to make these kinds of broad predictions for people.

One of the strange things about astrology, however, is you can never boil down what you say to technique. It can seem like it is just technique – when Pluto squares the Sun, you get a major empowerment – but it isn't. It is ultimately about the astrologer, and what is being whispered in her ear by the goddesses as she takes in the symbols. The technique has to be held lightly, because once you think you can pin down what is going to happen in this semi-literal way, you will find it stops working as a technique. I can almost guarantee that. It is strange. It is as though a trickster comes in, just to stop you pinning everything down and creating a kind of certainty, which is something humans love to do.

The psychologist Carl Jung, who was more of an astrologer than he let on, noticed this. At one point he observed that people who were in a romantic relationship with one another had the classic Sun-Moon interactions that one expects to regularly find. He began testing this result with a series of couples, and the result broke down. Magical reality was not going to be pinned down in this way.

There is no apparent reason that this breakdown should happen. In a way, it makes no sense. But from the point of view of the larger reality within which our tiny 'logical' reality exists, it makes perfect sense. Astrology is essentially about listening to what the gods are saying, we are oracles. We may use techniques to reach a symbolic place that is fitting for the information that we seek. But then we listen. That is the crucial bit. If we start thinking it is just about the technique, then we are no longer listening in that subtle way, so how can we possibly get the right information? This happened to me in 2020, when I got the result of the US Presidential election wrong. Some people love to slate me on Facebook when I get a prediction wrong, but I see no shame in it. The point is to learn from it. And if you can't make mistakes, you can't learn.

What I had noticed with political leaders is that generally they need major transits to propel them into power, and they tend to remain in power while they continue to have major transits. And then they fall from power once those transits are over. I had noticed this particularly with UK leaders, because they can go on and on, and they can leave anytime, unlike the US, where their tenure is more defined.

I had made a prediction in about 2003 that Tony Blair would be Prime Minister until about 2007/8, because at that point the series of hard Neptune transits to his MC then Moon then Sun would start to complete. This is not an exact art, because with outer planet transits, the major events can occur at any point within the period of the transit. I was right enough in the case of Blair, and I had been able to look back and see that it worked well too with Margaret Thatcher who had Pluto transits empowering her. And that too was interesting: Blair, who was known for 'spin', had been characterised by Neptune transits, whereas Thatcher, who was known for confrontation and killing off that which was outdated, was characterised by Pluto transits while in power.

I think the danger for me with this method was that it seemed almost to occur like clockwork. Barack Obama had originally been elected as Neptune was concluding its conjunction to his Asc, and it started squaring his Moon as he campaigned for his second term. As a method, it seemed to work pretty well.

With Donald Trump it was slightly different. I predicted he

would win the 2016 election before he had even declared himself a candidate. This wasn't based on major transits, because he didn't quite have any. And nor did his opponent, Hillary Clinton. But Trump's chart made such strong aspects to the US chart, while Hillary's made very few, that I predicted he would win. And even though he won fewer votes than Clinton, he won the election.

Now here is another thing: because I predicted Trump would win in 2016, there were people who assumed that I must therefore be a Trump supporter. You don't quite know what to say when people come out with things like this, it shows such a misunderstanding of how astrology works: that it is a disinterested craft, and it is not on the side of who you think is the 'good guy'. It is not on anyone's 'side', because the gods are not. They have much larger designs that we cannot even conceive of, and that is why it is good we cannot always get the predictions right, otherwise we would develop hubris.

Anyway, fast-forward four years, and Trump is up for re-election. He was in the middle of Neptune squaring his Sun and Moon, my rational self told me that he was probably going to lose the election, but my astrological method told me he would win. And the method was wrong. What his Neptune transit described was his loss of the election, and his descent into a cult leader who believed he had won and that it had been stolen from him.

So, this is why prediction can be a difficult thing. Yes, we need to centre it on the astrology and a particular method. But then we need to take circumstances into account. And then we need to listen to ourselves, and that is maybe the trickiest thing of all: how do we distinguish between what we want to happen, our prejudices if you like, and the voices of intuition? Going back to that panel of astrologers who almost unanimously predicted that Hillary Clinton would win the election, it seems to me clear that some of them were not able, in that case, to make this distinction. It doesn't mean they are not able to do so in other circumstances. But here was a situation where one outcome was not desired to a very high degree by maybe most astrologers. They found Trump repugnant. But disinterest, and therefore astrological accuracy, was lost.

It was probably one of the most challenging situations in which to practise astrology. It was maybe easier for me because I am from the UK. I think it was also easier for me because I don't generally identify with one political wing or the other. I think if these astrologers had watched and absorbed Jonathan Haidt's Ted talk, more of them might have been able to predict the outcome correctly.

The disinterest that astrology requires of us is a serious 'warrior' training, it could also be called 'impeccability'. Not many people have it. It requires exceptional self-awareness, that usually takes many years of practice. It is about who we are, it is about our whole being. The astrology itself is quite easy compared to this.

Not only is there a bit of a 'no-no' around prediction generally, there is an even bigger 'no-no' around predicting death for many astrologers. It is seen as seriously unethical. It is even treated as taboo by some, which you can tell is happening when people won't engage with your arguments, or they start making it personal. Of course, you don't want to 'spook' people, and if someone is liable to be spooked, you don't say it. Many people hear what they want to hear, and they may come back at you years later about predictions you have made, that miss out any qualifications, or nuances, you may have made around what you said.

But sometimes people want to know if they are liable to die at particular times, and I am always straight with them. I try to be straight with people about everything, always. I don't have a problem with death. As the philosopher Francis Bacon said 450 years ago,

"It is as natural to die as to be born."

But for me there have to be reasons that they might die, like a serious health condition. I have frequently, and accurately, predicted close relatives dying, because that can often be seen in your own chart. But again, only if they have serious health issues already, otherwise there is no reason to suppose it.

A couple of predictions to finish this chapter. As I've said, I like to keep the astrology simple, in order to maintain a felt sense of the symbolism. And I try to distance myself from any desire I have for a particular outcome (while not denying I have that desire.)

Below is the chart for the EU.

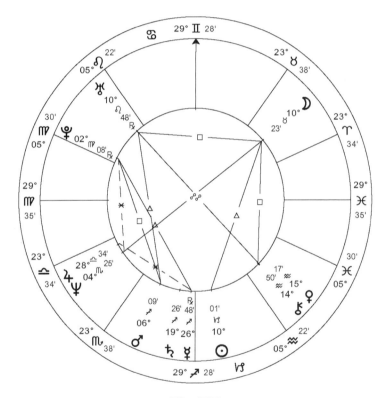

The EU

It first came into existence as an organisation (the EEC) in 1958, so that is the chart I am using. In the chart of a country, the Moon is the people (and the Sun the government). In the case of the EU, we can see the Moon either as the constituent peoples, or the member states. It is a very appropriate Moon: its nature, its reason for being there, is shared (8th house) prosperity (Taurus). Economics, in other words, is the real driver, from the point of view of the member states. In 2020/21, Uranus (separation) passed over the EU Moon, and the UK left the EU. It seems to works as a chart.

In 2024/25, Neptune will oppose the Ascendant and square the MC. The four Angles on the chart are our strongest points of connection to the planet. As I said earlier, I see the emphasis of the planets in signs as the inner course of our lives, and that of the houses (the Angles are the four main house cusps) as on outer events, the arenas of life that we find ourselves in. It is never as black and white as that, but we can be sure that when one of the two most powerful transformers, Neptune or Pluto (the most powerful because furthest from the earth) hard aspects all four Angles, that person or country will go through a fundamental shift in their lives, according to the signs involved, whether it is Neptune or Pluto, and the natures of the hard aspects involved (i.e., conjunction, square or opposition.)

But I am going to keep it simple. Pluto crossing these Angles in the late noughties corresponded to the fiscal crisis and the Greek bailout, when the EU was forced by circumstances to act centrally in a way that it hadn't before. That maybe gives us a clue to the meaning of the Neptune transit. Neptune and Pluto transits are different in nature, but they also have a lot in common (see Chapter 5.)

Whatever happens, it will involve the EU in some kind of dissolution and re-imagining of itself. This is the nature of Neptune, just as Pluto involves issues around power. The departure of the UK was a body-blow to the EU's vision of an integrated Europe, at least in the terms it had come to understand integration. And then the vaccine fiasco of 2021 showed that in this crisis, at least, the EU was not centralised enough to act effectively, nor federal enough for its member states to go their own way. The vision of unity was not working in practice.

These things take a few years to work through. But in the run-up to the Neptune transit, there was, effectively, a vote of no-confidence from the UK, followed by paralysis in a crisis. It has to decide which way it wants to go. If it was Pluto that was acting, I might say there would be an attempt to assert more control from the centre. Because it is Neptune, and because of what has happened, my prediction is that there will be some kind of unravelling at the centre, a loss of the old dream (Neptune) of unity, to be replaced by a vision that is more hard-edged, more practical and that allows member states to act more autonomously. This is affirmed by the presence of practical Saturn, which will hard aspect the EU Angles in 2025, and then over the following year will join Neptune in the sign of Aries, which also suggests a new vision.

My other prediction involves Northern Ireland, which came into existence on 7 Dec 1922.

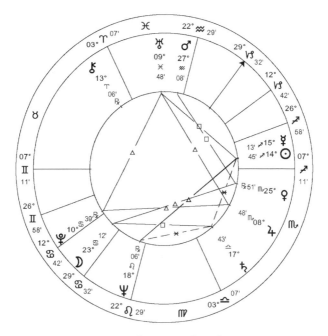

Northern Ireland

At the end of 2024, it will complete a long transit of Pluto, firstly opposite its Moon at 23 Cancer, and then conjoining its MC at 29 Capricorn. This transit began in earnest in 2020, with Pluto exactly opposing the Moon, as the negotiations for the UK to leave the EU showed that the status of NI in relation to the UK would be changing: there would be a customs border in the Irish seas between the UK and NI, but no customs border between the north and south of Ireland. In other words, the UK leaving the EU meant NI moving closer to Eire and away from the UK. This was of course a huge challenge to the people and their sense of who they are, as evinced by the transit of Pluto opposite to the Moon. There have been decades of bitter warfare over precisely this issue.

It would seem that the writing is on the wall. The Pluto opposite Moon transit reflected a shift in the balance of power within the population, away from those who favour being part of the UK, and towards those who want a united Ireland. This shift found practical expression in early 2021, as Saturn made its final crossing to the MC and the new trade arrangements came into place, with the predicted disruption of trade with mainland UK, that changed the place of NI in the world (MC). As Pluto crosses the MC in 2023/24, this process will deepen, but it will have a natural quality, as Neptune trines the Moon and gives the people a new vision of who they are. My prediction is therefore that by the end of 2024, as Pluto moves definitively into Aquarius, Northern Ireland will have re-aligned itself more closely with Eire, and less so with the UK. Whether this will, at that stage, constitute a full re-unification, remains to be seen. Probably not quite. The Protestants will require some kind of special status to keep them on board. But after that it will only be a matter of time.

Chapter 4

Relationships

Along with death, another area I try to be straight in, is relationships. If someone comes to see me because they are having problems in their marriage or relationship, it is a fairly safe bet that its days are numbered, and that is without even looking at the astrology. And sure enough, there are always some major indicators when I come to look at the chart. The person is usually changing, a new phase of their life is trying to open up, and the relationship has up till now set boundaries around who they are. The partner needs them to be a particular way, and we have also in turn needed the partner to be a particular way, and that involves an unconscious process of projection and self-editing that occurs right at the start of the relationship. When that has occurred, it is called 'falling in love'.

What sometimes happens, however, is that one person starts to wake up to who they are in a deeper kind of way, and the other person doesn't. That is why the relationship usually has to come to an end. The pressure that creates – and these things are nearly always messy – can often be precisely what is needed for us to start to value that new way of being that is emerging, that has probably always been there, but not given its proper place. And it is usually tied up with what gives our life meaning, what it is that is at the centre of what you might call our metaphysical quest.

Mars and Venus are the planets that begin relationships. Mars in a woman's chart, for example, may describe the type of man she is attracted to. And Venus for a man. But the long-term partner is often described by the Sun or the Moon respectively in a woman's or a man's chart. I don't know how this works with gay people, because I haven't had many come to me for readings.

When we go through a hard transit from Pluto or Neptune

to the Sun or Moon – and these tend to be the biggest, most life-transforming, transits – long-term relationships are often one of the casualties. This is because the Sun and Moon play such a large part in who we are, they are often to some extent projected onto the partner, and a transit is a time of waking up to the next stage in our lives, a time of claiming that which has hitherto been unconscious.

The end of as long-term relationship can be one of the biggest, most transformative events in our lives, drawn out and messy as it usually is, with lots of prevarication, lots of attempts to keep it working, along the way.

There is the saying that men are from Mars and women are from Venus, and it has become a bit of a cliché, but that is because there is truth in it. Not only this, but at mid-life men and women start to swap round. A lot of men start to become more relational and connected to their feelings, while many women start to know more what they want for themselves, and feel less obliged to take care of everyone around them.

This kind of awakening can be a useful lens through which to look at relationship difficulties. It is a very important process, because it is not just about acquiring a few more character attributes: it is about finding one's soul, as if for the first time. The psychologist Carl Jung talked about this process in terms of the anima and animus, the female and male contra-sexual sides within us.

Most of the people who come to me for readings are women, so I am more familiar with their process in this respect. Even though we might not admit it, and it is maybe politically incorrect to do so from a feminist point of view, men and women do often divide the psyche up between them in quite traditional ways. And the side of the psyche that the partner carries for us is by definition quite undeveloped, and we therefore seek a parental figure in the partner who will take care of us in that respect: whether it is a father to protect us against a big, threatening world, or a mother to take care of us and soothe us and nurture us. It is usually far from clear to us that this is what we are doing when we begin a relationship – or we probably wouldn't go there – but taking a long perspective, it is often precisely the route we need to our eventual awakening.

All this is quite 'normal'. In a way, in the first part of our adult lives, it is enough for us to learn to live out one side of the psyche. The other half can come later. It is not just social conditioning. Women really are better at taking care of young children: when a baby is born all sorts of powerful instincts come alive in them, that have nothing to do with social conditioning, and that do not do so in men. And it means they are better at being 'agreeable' (which is one of the big Five Psychological Traits that have been agreed on, through research, in recent decades, along with Openness, Conscientiousness, Neuroticism and Extraversion). But by virtue of being more 'agreeable', it is harder to fight for what you want for yourself and piss other people off in the process. This is something that men, who are less personally connected to others, by and large, find easier. And then at mid-life, all this starts to change. Of course, it is never so simple and schematic, but there is enough truth in it, coming out of the many readings I have done for people, to make a valid generalisation.

I see it almost like clockwork in the charts of mothers, that as their youngest child reaches the next stage of independence, such as going to school for the first time, so too does the mother have a transit that describes a greater degree of independence and possibility for her too. There is, if you like, a long process of Mars coming to life as the children grow older.

But then we get the 'mid-life crisis', which is when Mars and Venus (as well as other astrological factors) get serious, and which can go on for years, and which Jung describes in terms of starting to discover, and live from, one's own values, instead of those of the society around us. This happened to Jung from his late 30s onwards, during the First World War. He talks about himself in these terms, as having built a successful professional reputation: he had a wife, family and wealth too, everything one could wish for. But then he found himself withdrawing. All that no longer held the same compulsion for him, and he went on his journey into the Unconscious, which he describes in his *Red Book*, much of which is an account of his conversations with Philemon, who is what we might call a Spirit Guide. He later said that everything he had to say that was of value came from that period in his life.

It is a profound experience, this meeting with our deeper selves, and that is often what we are guiding people through when they come for a reading under major transits: their old lives are perhaps falling apart, and they are maybe desperately trying to hang on to that old life with one hand, while on the other reaching out to that new element which is calling to them irresistibly, yet causing them so much misery as it calls into question the lives they have hitherto built for themselves.

There is a book called *The Middle Passage* by James Hollis, a Jungian analyst, that describes very well this mid-life process that can go on and on. In a way, it never stops. There is a constant call to live from that daemon within, to keep moving life forward. It requires that we step outside of received values and live by our own values – or, maybe more accurately, the transpersonal values of the daimon – and that can mean learning to ignore the judgement of others. Jung himself had a mistress, and did not conceal the fact. It was outrageous in his day, but he did not care what people thought. One can question the wisdom of that second relationship with Toni Wolff, but that is another issue.

Aquarius is the classic sign that is able to break the rules, and Jung had Aquarius Rising. What Aquarius often has to learn is that one needs to earn the right to break the rules: your radical vision doesn't amount to much if you can't also be part of society and make some sort of peace with its rules.

A fascinating psychological diversion: Jung and Freud were the two towering figures of early psychoanalysis. Jung was Freud's Crown Prince, his heir apparent, but he eventually broke with Freud over the nature of the unconscious. Typical Aquarian rebel!

Freud had Sun in Taurus with Scorpio Rising. His psychology emphasises the libido, the instincts, which are strongly associated with those two signs. Jung had Sun in Leo with Aquarius Rising. His psychology emphasises individuation, the unfoldment of the Self, which is very descriptive of the Leo-Aquarius axis. Seeing this was one of those *wow!* moments that astrology so often provides. And they both have Sun and Uranus in the 7th House: they were both ground-breaking (Uranus) counsellors/therapists (7th House). I associate the 6th House more with healing, and the 7th with the ability to form relationship and enter another's world.

Astrology can be very good at helping us to understand and relativise, rather than dividing into right and wrong. In the case of Freud and Jung, their psychological theories were an expression of how they were individually built. There are other ways of looking at the psyche that are just as valid. And it is the same with Mercury in the chart: it shows the way we learn individually. The school system tends to be one-size fits all, by necessity, and if that method doesn't suit you, you can spend the rest of your life thinking you are stupid.

I am writing this book as it comes to me. I know I have plenty to say, and I am letting the topics I cover present themselves organically. Much how I do readings. We have moved from relationships to mid-life crises, because difficulty or ending in relationship is often associated with that mid-life process. It seems like time now to say something about the nature of the major transits that are associated with these types of crisis and transition.

Chapter 5

My Neptune and Pluto Initiations

Under a major transit you (ideally) start to listen to yourself in a new way, maybe listen to yourself for the first time. In the first part of our lives, the emphasis is often on listening to the voices of our parents and the wider collective and what it wants us to be. And there is nothing wrong with that, it is quite normal. As a child, it is in many ways necessary. And many people are happy to live their whole lives out in this manner. Who they are is defined for them by received values, and in conforming to those values, in succeeding according to those values, a kind of contentment is achieved.

They are comfortable in their own skins – though it wouldn't surprise me if there is always some kind of niggle around something larger wanting to get in, for that is the nature of life. The major transits still happen, but for people who don't want to be awake, who do not even know there is such a thing, the transits seem to pass them by. You can usually see major outward events that correspond to such times, and they are always opportunities for inner change, but you can never tell if someone is going to take up that challenge. The mid-life crisis, which we were exploring above, is one of the archetypal times when this process happens.

The element of awakening, or the desire to do so, is a mysterious thing that is not in the chart. If someone comes to see you for a reading, the chances are that desire is active, and that is why they have come to see you, and our job is to shed some light on it. There are other people change very little during their lives. Life is perhaps a straightforward thing for them. They maybe know what they want, and think they know who they are, from a young age, and they simply get on with it, with the usual amount of difficulty and suffering along the way.

Another term for these major transits is Initiation. Something new from Spirit, from the gods, from the deeper Self, is trying to come into consciousness. That can never be a simple-add on, it always involves a fundamental re-arrangement of who we are, and that is why such times are so challenging. Change is difficult, we fear it.

That was why in the UK there was so much grief from 2016 onwards about the decision to leave the EU. Rights and wrongs apart – and I am not sure there were any – it was going to involve a big change in many people's idea of what collective they belonged to, and these things go deep. My view, as an astrologer who sees the value and necessity of change, is that these sorts of shake-ups in who we think we are (which is ultimately illusory) are good for us. They allow something new to come in to our habitual way of being.

There are certain major changes that correspond to the biological stages of life, but which also reflect inner changes. And there are other major changes which are less biologically determined. In a traditional society, these more regular changes are marked by ceremony and by initiation. Any new phase, where something new enters our consciousness, is an initiation. Birth and death are initiations, in which you cannot know what is coming next. Puberty is a time of initiation, in which we begin to make the transition from child to adult. From *The Philosopher's Secret Fire* pp91-7 by Patrick Harpur,

> "A traditional puberty rite usually contains an element of ordeal, and spirit vision/induction into the tribal myths, and acceptance as an adult by the community. For the Sioux in North America, for example, the boy is firstly put through a Sweatlodge (which is characterised by intense heat) and then immediately brought to a hilltop where he is placed in a cramped vision pit for days without food and water. At the end of this time he will, hopefully, have been granted a vision and been turned from a boy to a man"

We do not, uniquely, have such rites of passage in our culture, nor do we (again, uniquely) have a prevailing mythology that provides meaning. It may well mean that many boys and girls take a lot longer reaching adulthood, if at all.

However, it is not my purpose to bemoan this situation. We have what we have and let us not compare ourselves unfavourably, it doesn't usually help. Young people *do* attempt to initiate themselves, albeit without necessarily realising it. It is a natural thing. And life has a way of initiating us anyway.

As Harpur continues:

> *"During a special sacred time of about two weeks in summer, young European initiates fly to the Otherworld where they inhabit a liminal zone between land and sea. By day they are 'cooked' by a process of frying under a scorching sun, and periodically plunged into cold water; by night they undergo an elaborate Dionysian ritual involving an orgy of wine, dancing and sex. They call this a 'Mediterranean holiday'."*

I would add the drug 'Ecstasy' to Harpur's account, the illegality of which adds an initiatory edge, taking one outside permitted norms.

Criminal behaviour, dangerous driving, risk-taking (I still shudder at the blind corner on which I impatiently overtook someone when I was 20) are often also driven by this craving for initiation.

It is worth looking back and seeing where your own need for initiation took you as a teenager and young adult, and the new elements that may have entered your consciousness, and their implications for your future. And, as astrologers, it is especially worth looking back and seeing what the transits were at such transformative, and often very difficult, times. And we can find common themes or threads of awakening running through our lives. Maybe it was Pluto when we were a teenager, then maybe Neptune hard-aspected the same point 10 or 15 years later, each with its own flavour and its own initiation, but building on what came before. In this way you can build an astro-biography, a history of the ways in which the gods have initiated you over the course of your life, the inevitability, the fate of that, and yet within that, the deep choices about who you were going to be that you were always being prompted to make, and which lay at the heart of those changes. This sort of analysis, and the perspective it gives, lies for me right at the heart of astrology.

Here is an abbreviated version of my own initiatory story, beginning with Neptune.

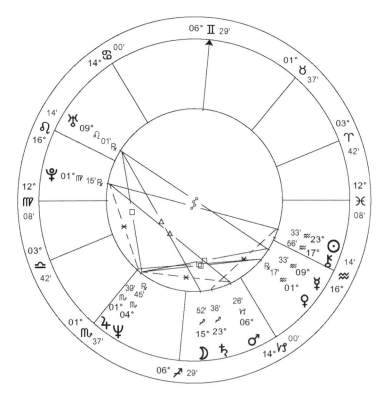

Author's Chart

In early 1973, as I turned 15, Neptune crossed the bottom of my chart, the IC, the roots of who I was. Over the previous year or two (these transits nearly always begin before the exact aspects occur) I had become painfully aware that I did not feel my life to be my own, that my future had been decided for me by my parents, and as the eldest son I was to follow my father into the business he had established. Neptune can put us into a dream, even into a kind of madness; but he can also awaken us from a dream. In this case, I was awakening from the dream of childhood (the IC concerns early family life), in which we have little sense of who we are as a separate individual. Jung describes this process for himself in his *Memories, Dreams, Reflections,* and also in the 1959 BBC Freeman interview (which I highly recommend, and can be found on YouTube). He describes it as a sudden awakening to who he was, in which he realised that before this he had had no existence, he was just part of the surroundings, but that now he knew 'that I am'.

Now here is where you are going to have to trust me. I wrote the above (apart from the last sentence) without looking at Jung's chart. I just thought he would make a good illustration of what I was talking about in the case of my own life. And what do we find? In 1887, when he was 12 years old, about the time of his awakening, Neptune passed over the IC of his chart, just as it did for me. I love it when astrology provides such unbidden synchronicities. It shows that the gods are watching over us, urging us on in our endeavours.

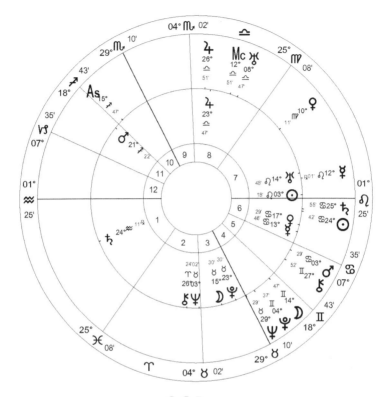

C.G.Jung

If this was an astrology group, people would be immediately chipping in with the other transits and maybe progressions too that Jung was having at the time. That is all well and good, especially perhaps the conjunction of Saturn to his Descendant: when Saturn is also operative, the inner changes that the outer planets are describing – or causing, depending on your point of view – tend to find concrete form. For myself, the run-up to Neptune crossing my IC was when I had the awakening, and in that time, Saturn also opposed my IC. But I always think that when considering these transits, it can be good to make the hard outer-planet transit the fundamental one, see that as the real nature of what is happening, and to just sit with that, feel it for a while, before bringing in progressions and other transits, which will add supportive information. Otherwise, the primary nature of the event can get lost.

In my early teens I was experiencing this transit as a painful event, as something that had gone wrong. But that is often the way of things with transformative transits. Something is trying to wake up, and that often begins with an experience of the limitations of our present situation, which is often uncomfortable if not worse. It was, when I look back, a natural process for a boy who had a vocation inside of him that he did not yet know about. If I had been built differently, there would not have been a problem. My father's desire for me to follow him into the business – a natural enough thing – would not have been experienced as a constriction, but as an opportunity. Of course, it was tied in with his own needs, and he was not treating his son as a separate individual, but that is just how normal, unconscious humanity works. If we don't expect too much of people who live in an unconscious way, we shall save ourselves a lot of grief, and be able also to be more at peace with who we are ourselves.

The next major Neptune transit was a few years later, when I was 19, an exact conjunction to my Moon in Sagittarius. Despite my sense of conflict, which continued right through my teens, I began training to be a veterinary surgeon, my father's line of business. After five months of it, I realised I did not want to go on with it, and it was like a large burden being lifted from my shoulders. It was an emotional experience, as you would expect with the Moon. Like the previous Neptune awakening, the emphasis was more on what I did not want rather than what I did want, but it was one more stage in the process. Behind it all, pushing it, was the sign of Sagittarius: a need for a connection to, a faith in, some deeper dimension.

In the year following the exact conjunction to the Moon, when I was 20, I spent several months regularly ingesting psilocybin mushrooms, several thousand of which a group of us had found in a field. This is classic Neptune territory, and I experienced the highs and lows: the god like states, and the darker initiation into my shadow side, which was very painful, but a necessary part of becoming whole. I came out of that period very different: I now knew absolutely that the commercial trajectory, or even anything 'normal', was not for me, and that I would need to be doing something with my life that answered my unformulated calling.

This was also a crisis for me, which is often a part of these Pluto and Neptune transits. A crisis essentially involves hanging on to the old, despite the pressure from the new, until eventually there is resolution – which usually means giving in to that which wants to be born, and surrendering the old. In my case, the demand for a successful professional career from my father and the education I had been through seemed absolute; it seemed unthinkable to do anything else. And yet I had to.

The approach to psychology known as Psychosynthesis talks in terms of a deeper Self that at certain periods in life pushes to express itself more fully; a new element starts to come into consciousness, and that causes a crisis, because the whole personality has to be re-arranged around this new element, and the old and familiar needs to be let go of. This model describes well what the major Pluto and Neptune crises can be like, and because these planets are slow moving, the crises can be drawn out over some years.

Neptune transits are often associated with confusion, a time when nothing seems to work or to make sense, like being in a swamp in the mist. I think that is true, but I also think the confusion – which I certainly experienced during my whole period at university – is to do with the old dissolving, and us not being ready to let it go. The deeper sense of vocation, and the concomitant re-imagining of our lives, which is at the heart of Neptune transits, is not swamp-like and confused. It may not be formulated, we may not be ready to know exactly what it is (if indeed we ever fully know), but I think it is always there to be listened to, it is always in that sense clear. Many transits have this sense of confusion, of things not being clear, around them, but within that there is something new in ourselves to be listened to, which is the whole point of what is happening.

The old and the new between them create the sense of crisis, and this can be clear as a bell when we look at someone's chart. It is often our job to explain to clients what is happening, to hold their hand as it were and re-assure them that they are not going crazy, even though other people might think so. I had this experience myself 35 years later, as Neptune made his next round of hard aspects to my Angles, Moon and Saturn, of a partner being convinced I had gone 'nuts' as I awoke in new ways and broke the unconscious deal between us.

A couple of years later, when I was 23, Neptune conjoined my Saturn in Sagittarius, and I got involved with a Buddhist group. The symbolism was perfect: Saturn (organisation) and Sagittarius (religion.) This Buddhist group was a bit like an 18-year refugee camp, a holding centre for me, while my metaphysical quest took root, and I was able eventually to head off with it on my own, so to speak. It had its light and its dark, so while on the one hand Neptune was continuing to awaken me to my deeper calling, he was also leading me by the nose, deceiving me in a necessary way.

Neptune is often associated with deception, and in ordinary situations his presence may reflect that things are not what they seem. Do not sign a legal contract, for example, while Neptune is in a challenging aspect to Mercury. But this is not a 'bad' aspect. Astrology is not about good and bad, not nowadays anyway. Sometimes it is. If a door-to-door salesman visits you under Mercury square Neptune, you might be well-advised to say no to whatever great deal he is offering you.

But more often the challenging aspects are an invitation to inspect, to analyse and maybe get to know ourselves better. With the legal contract, Mercury square Neptune says look at it again, what might you have overlooked? Neptune also says wait, there may be things which become apparent later which are not so clear now. And if we are fully paying attention to ourselves and to the situation, we do not need the planets. We will have our own awareness, our own skills, our own intuitions to guide us. The planets are an aid to our own judgement, rather than a substitute for it.

However, we can in the last analysis never second-guess the gods. They have their own reasons, and Neptune may sometimes simply blindside us, and afterwards it may be that we can look back and see there was something in that situation that we have learnt from, that has changed us, that would not have occurred if we had not stumbled in. Or sometimes, with the best will in the world, we are deceived under Neptune, and there seems to be no reason for it. But that's just life. Our consciousness is tiny, the consciousness of the universe is vast. There is only ever a limited amount we can know, however open we are. Neptune is that vast ocean of awareness that is also the universe. Matter and awareness are the objective and subjective dimensions respectively of the same thing. If we were to meet Neptune or indeed any of the planets in their fullness, they would destroy us, for we are talking about gods, and we can only take so much.

"Humankind cannot bear very much reality"

So, Neptune led me into a tradition that would help my metaphysical quest take root. I was surprised by how strong that quest was, I had up till then thought it would be a part-time thing. I was swept into it. In a sense, I was maddened. This is how Liz Greene describes the mythology behind Pisces in her book *The Astrology of Fate*, which contains a great section on what she considers relevant mythologies for each sign. The modern ruler of Pisces is Neptune. Liz Greene reckons there is a good case for the wine god Dionysus being a more appropriate figure (p 261).

King Pentheus was driven mad by Dionysus because he rejected his rites, and then torn apart by his entourage of female furies. There is much that can be drawn out of this story, but for now we are holding the idea that Neptune/Dionysus maddens us under his transits. This is a stronger, more visceral way of saying deception. Deception is a mental or cognitive attribute. Being maddened is the whole of you being swept along. Possession by the god is another word for it. And it is in many ways a profoundly good thing to be taken over in this way.

When we surrender to the spirit in this way – which all outer planet transits ask of us, each in their own manner – then it is as if we are taken care of at all levels. We are honouring the daimon. We get gifts and blessings, and we get lessons as well. In my joining this Buddhist group, Neptune was also leading me into a situation where I would come up against the desire of the teacher to have everyone thinking like he did, and the need for me to eventually break away from that; to find, for the first time, my own deeper autonomy, my ability to trust my own inner guidance and not rely on received values and opinions, which is the normal human way of operating, however much people deny it. It was a necessary deception that had my long-term learnings in mind. The outer planets have a perspective on us that we cannot possibly have, which is why we need to simply trust them. That trust is something we build over the years, and in this way become a 'hollow bone' for the gods. And probably brilliant astrologers too! But it is a long process.

So that, put briefly, was the series of awakenings and crises and maddenings (the psilocybin mushrooms were a maddening too) that Neptune led me through as he hard-aspected my Angles, Moon and Saturn over a ten-year period. He took me from a place of awakening to my separate existence in my early teens, all the way through to a life of Buddhist practice in my early twenties.

At the time of writing, I am at the end of this same series of transits, but 90 degrees on and 35 years later. It has also been a very transformative – and challenging – period, with some similar themes. Neptune is starting to square my Saturn, and instead of joining a Buddhist group, I am writing books. Saturn gives form, and it is therefore good to have him involved at the end of a series of transits, when it is time to start living all those changes we have been through. Both now and 35 years ago I was beginning to give long-term form to the calling that had been growing in me for the years of the transits. This time, however, the emphasis is on something coming purely from within, without the external structure in terms of teachings and people that I needed all those years ago.

When people are having major transits, there may well be a series they are having over a long period, and it is worth taking this bigger view, to cast light on what is happening now, and to see what was unfolding in past transits, in the light of the present. You can also look at the last time an outer planet hard-aspected those points in the chart, and see what themes were raised then, and how they reflect on what is happening now. There is so much you can dig up in this way.

The softer aspects can be used too – the sextiles and trines – if you want a really detailed analysis. I stick to the hard aspects, because they tend to be the most challenging, and therefore most transformative, transits. And it keeps the picture a bit simpler, it shows the bare bones more clearly.

I hope that in looking at those early transits of mine, something of the nature of Neptune has come through. I prefer to start with examples and let the theory as to the nature of the planet emerge organically from that. Let us move on in the same way to Pluto and his initiations, and also hopefully to a comparison between Neptune and Pluto transits. Fast forward ten years to the early 90s. I had been busy living the life that Neptune had thrown me into aged 23, and Pluto had begun to square my Sun.

And I ground to a halt. The type of Buddhism I was around

was quite evangelical, and there was a lot of emphasis on running its various institutions as a path to Enlightenment. I was very good at this, even though, in my heart of hearts, it wasn't really what I wanted to be doing. As Pluto came to within a couple of degrees of the square to my Sun, I started to experience a darkness coming into me and dragging me down. How else would you expect a Pluto transit to begin? After all, the classic mythology behind him is his abduction of Proserpina into the Underworld, and I was being abducted – the first stage in his transformational process.

Here is the mythology. Pluto, Lord of the Underworld, abducted Proserpina (Greek Persephone), young daughter of the fertility goddess Ceres. Ceres was left distraught, unable to find her daughter and not knowing what had happened to her. In her distress, the permanent state of summer that had existed on Earth came to an end, the leaves fell from the trees, the sun cooled and life withdrew. Eventually, Helios, the Sun, who sees everything, came to Ceres' aid and told him what had happened to Proserpina, who had been forcibly married to, and in some versions raped, by Pluto.

After some negotiation, it was agreed that Proserpina would return for six months of the year to be with her mother, and for the other six months she would return to be with her husband. And so, for half the year, Ceres rejoiced while her daughter was with her, and summer returned to the earth. And for the six months she was with Pluto, winter returned. This is how the seasons came about.

It is just the same with the individual human life: there are periods of activity and expansion, and periods of withdrawal and re-dreaming of who we are. It is when we resist those natural cycles (as we often do) that the trouble starts. During the Covid lockdowns, practically the whole world went into a rare period of withdrawal. Maybe in some way that was one of the functions, one of the reasons for the virus, in a one-sidedly extraverted world?

In the case of Ceres, Jupiter, king of the gods, had given Pluto permission to abduct Proserpina, because he understood that Ceres would never let her daughter go willingly. This reflects a sometimes brutal law of life: that it must move on. Proserpina was inducted forcibly into the next stage of life – from girl to woman – because her mother was not going to let that happen. Because of her resistance, Earth turned to a wasteland.

In this story, Ceres represents nature in its habitual form, and the resistance it has to change, which is probably something we all experience for ourselves. And in doing that, there is usually something in ourselves that we are ignoring, that we think we can overlook for the sake of everything else. The planet Pluto was discovered at the same time as nuclear energy, in which immense power is harnessed from a tiny source. It is the same with the astrological Pluto: the tiny seed of something we were overlooking proves to have immense power that can revolutionise our lives. And when its time has come, it becomes an offer you cannot refuse, as the Godfather put it. The more strongly you resist, the harder Pluto will push back. He will make you ill, he will destroy your life, you may even die in the process. Things will not start to come right until we listen to ourselves in a new way.

When Pluto began calling me with his darkness in mid-1991, when I was 33, I resisted for about nine months. I was busily and successfully heading up a network of communities and businesses and teaching centres. It was giving me a lot of kudos, but in a way all I was doing was being the type of person, an 'achiever', that I had been brought up to be, and that I had thought I was getting away from when I took up Buddhist practice.

The philosopher Nietzsche said:

"Beware that, when fighting monsters, you yourself do not become

a monster... for when you gaze long into the abyss, the abyss gazes also into you."

A monster is putting it strongly, but in fighting what I had been trained to be, I had become it, and I felt deeply dislocated from myself. But still I continued, because of my belief in the path I was following, and the compulsion of my habits. Pluto is himself a monster, but what he teaches us is that monsters are not monsters, not if we make friends with them, instead of fighting them. He was inducting me into a very different way of being with myself.

But first he had to make it impossible for me to continue as I had been – a very wilful, heady way of being, based too much on other people's ideas. It began with a sense of dark depression that would sometimes creep up on me. And a sense of pain, that if life was like this, I didn't really want to continue. I kept it at bay, but then my energy crashed. It wasn't tiredness, it was more a sense that the life-force had gone, the plug had been pulled. This was Pluto showing me that it wasn't me that was in control, it was him, it was something deeper in myself, and it had decided to press the 'off' switch, and there was nothing I could do about it.

Although I experienced this as a very uncomfortable constriction, I was in fact being initiated into something profound: that control over our lives, and over who we are, is illusory, that really something much bigger is calling the shots and steering our lives. We are like a small boat on the ocean, imagining we are directing where we are going, when in fact it the deeper ocean currents that are taking us where they will. Ever since this time I have been learning to trust in this deeper design, and to put down the burden of planning and directing my life, and learnt to follow whatever it is that seems to want to happen next.

I discontinued the role I had been fulfilling, and for the next four years, nothing I tried worked. It was time to stop and listen, which I did for much of the time, but the old me that was heady and driven, and felt like it was worthless unless it was 'achieving' something, did not go quietly. But each time, Pluto would stop him by pulling the plug on my energy.

What did work, however, was my growing interest in Shamanism and Astrology. Both of these took me to an inner place that the type of Buddhism I had been practising never could. And when I followed these two interests, I had all the energy I needed. Pluto was initiating me into a very different way of being, a way of listening to myself that I had not previously given proper value. And that was where my energy lay. And my 'power', which is also one meaning of Pluto.

Shamanism begins with the experience that the natural world is alive, inspirited, sacred, and that we belong to it. The Buddhism I had been practising was based on a paradigm of transcendence: the path involved ascending through higher and higher levels of consciousness until Enlightenment is reached, leaving this world, which is created through a combination of greed, hatred and ignorance, far behind. After this point, you will no longer be reborn. It was the same paradigm as Christianity, in which the world was the creation of the Devil, and Heaven was where it was really at. Buddhism doesn't have to be presented in these terms, but the renunciative emphasis of its institutional forms easily leads to that.

For me, this idea that the natural world is alive was intoxicating. It is also a very natural idea, but it is one that we have been increasingly forgetting in the West for the last 2500 years. (See *The Dream of the Cosmos* by Anne Baring, p99, where the author points the finger firmly at Plato and his over-emphasis on rationality, which was foundational for western civilisation.)

I call it the Great Forgetting. Christianity was one stage in that. Science, with its separation of mind and body, and its resulting technology that treats the natural world as a 'thing' to be exploited, is the current Forgetting. So, Shamanism had, for me, an intoxicating flavour, of a return to wholeness. The transcendent model of Buddhism had made me ill, to the point where I could do very little, but it was also an illness that was within the wider culture. As time went on, my energy loss seemed if anything to deepen, and I felt as though I was going through a major operation in which my very innards were being reworked. This is the psychological depth at which Pluto can work on and re-shape us, if we allow him to.

The western esoteric tradition, to which Astrology belongs, has the model of ascension through higher and higher spheres. Pluto, who lives in the Underworld, which is both visceral and earthy, is a corrective to this model. Pluto shows us that all is within us, if we learn to listen and to trust. It is a model of immanence, which allows for the natural world to be sacred, instead of something to be transcended.

What Pluto was initiating me into, most of all, was my own inner guide. He was saying you no longer need a teacher and a set of teachings to find your way, everything you need is within. Learn to trust that. This is what a good teacher does: helps people to the point where they can trust that guidance from within. Or from the gods, depending on how you like to look at it.

In my experience, many teachers want you to follow them, rather than your guidance from within. They will never say this, of course, and probably do not themselves believe that they want followers. But it happens as soon as you have a teacher and a group of people. It happens as much because the people attending want/need to be followers, as it does because the teacher needs them. It is a natural thing, for it can take a long time to reach that point of autonomy, where we are just relying on our own connection to the gods. A good teacher will find ways of handing the projection back. They can live with your disappointment that they are not the perfect being that you had projected onto them. It seems to be rare, however, for people to admit this dynamic in themselves, from either side of the fence. A teacher will always say they want their pupils to be independent, and the pupils will always say they are independent. There is no shame in admitting to it, however, and it means it can then be addressed. This is Pluto's Underworld, where we can admit straightforwardly to the aspects of ourselves that might be seen as shameful above ground, so to speak.

During most of the 90s, Pluto was busy demolishing me as I had been, and creating a space for me to listen to myself in a new, more authentic way. Or rather, I was learning to co-operate with Pluto in this work, which I think is the proper relationship with outer planets. Pluto lives deep underground, and through my calling towards shamanism, I was developing a connection with Earth and with my body that was giving me a stronger foundation in myself. The model of transcendence, of attaining higher states of consciousness, is a form of spiritual bypass, and it leaves you open to being controlled by others, because you do not have proper roots in yourself. Medieval Christianity was founded on spiritual bypass: it centres around trying to become 'good', while assigning your corporeal existence to the Devil.

Spiritual bypass is defined in Wikipedia as a

"tendency to use spiritual ideas and practices to sidestep or avoid facing unresolved emotional issues, psychological wounds, and unfinished developmental tasks."

Pluto is a collective planet. He is not visible to the naked eye, he comes from somewhere bigger, more mysterious. It is as though he was discovered at a time when the old religious form, Christianity, was breaking down, and it was becoming more possible to acknowledge the earth and the body as sacred again. And Pluto is an agent of that.

Pluto was in Scorpio and Sagittarius in the 90s, through both of which he moves quickly (for him). Before I knew it, Pluto had finished squaring my Sun in late Aquarius and was moving on to conjoin my IC in early Sagittarius. And in 1998 it was if a nuclear bomb exploded. I also had my Uranus opposition, the classic 'mid-life crisis' transit, awakening me, like flashes of lightning across the sky, illuminating the landscape in new ways, giving me a very different perspective on the Buddhism I had been engaged in for so many years. But underlying that was the new foundation that Pluto had been slowly building for the previous seven years, that gave me the wherewithal to absorb the Uranian insights.

Pluto and Neptune have been in a long sextile with each other, so that whatever Neptune does to us, Pluto will also do a while later. In my case, Neptune crossed my IC in my early teens, and Pluto did the same 25 years later. Neptune awoke me to my individual existence, by revealing the expectations others had for me, and my existential discomfort around that, the sense that my life had been stolen from me. Pluto enabled me at last to claim that individual existence, to ignore who others wanted me to be, and to trust my guidance from within. Or at least, to begin to. It was flip-flop process for some years, as these things often are. It was the ideas in my own head, as much as anything, about who I 'should' be, that came from my childhood, that I was beginning to definitively renounce.

I often think about the differences between Pluto and Neptune transits. They are, in my experience, equally transformative. And that is because they are about equidistant from the Sun at present. Eventually Pluto will move further out again – his orbit is very elliptical – and it is arguable that his transits will then become more powerful than those of Neptune. Let us see. I went through the same series of Neptune transits from 2013 onwards, but 90 degrees on, that had occurred from my teens onwards. So, there are all sorts of points of comparison to be made here, between the Neptune transits themselves, and between Pluto and Neptune.

I have found the flavour of Pluto transits to be more brutal. There are things we need to see, and aspects of ourselves to be claimed – our 'power' – and he will put us through difficult, confrontational situations in order to facilitate that. In the case of Pluto conjoining my IC (and by the same token, opposing my MC, who I was in the world), I found myself quite publicly pointing out the limitations of the Buddhist group that had been my life for so long. I went through a lot of fear and self-doubt as I did this, but I felt I had no choice. And it was precisely how I forged, gained confidence in that new level of inner guidance that had awoken. Ever since I have found myself to be the guy who says the things that no-one else dare say, and that has continued to shape me. It gives you a lot of trust in yourself when you are able to do this, and I think Pluto loves it, for he stands for what is real behind the social niceties and cover-ups.

I reserved judgement for many years on the nature of Neptune transits, until I had sufficient experience of them myself. What you read in books can only tell you so much. Books can point you in the right direction, but really, we know nothing about Pluto or Neptune, or indeed any of the planets, until we have experienced them at work. That may be through a strong natal placement, or it may be by transit, or through closely observing other people. The series of Neptune transits I experienced from 2013 onwards put me in a better position to comment. The main theme for me in this series was leaving a long-term relationship, and in-so-doing experiencing myself in new ways, finding a wholeness that was new, in which the 'feminine' in me was no longer there to be carried for me by a woman. The emphasis was less on claiming a power within me, as had been the case with Pluto, and more on a gradual awakening to something soulful, the 'anima', with plenty of floundering and uncertainty along the way, as one would expect from Neptune.

What is this floundering and uncertainty and even confusion that we classically experience under Neptune transits? I think it is the same sort of confusion as is pointed to in the Moon card in the Tarot. What I think it really is, is that something deep within us is being gestated, and it is not ready to be born. It may be some years before it is ready to be born. The confusion arises largely, I think, because we do not tune into that and surrender to it, but try to carry on as before. We keep trying to make our lives work in the old way, and of course they can't, so we can end up despondent and in a state of confusion. It is not confusion, however, to say that we do not know what we are doing with our lives right now. It is a simple statement of fact, and there is nothing 'wrong' with that unless you view clarity as a necessity.

Unless we can live without clarity, unless we can live with 'negative capability', then we will not be able to hear the gods. And it will be harder for the new gifts of Neptune, which also start to reveal themselves during our time of 'confusion', to come into consciousness. This applies also to Pluto transits: when we are in his wasteland, when we have been abducted, his new gifts will also be revealing themselves at the same time. Nothing is ever cut and dried in the transformational process. It can be a useful summary of the difference between these transits to say that under Pluto, we are abducted (like Proserpina), while under Neptune we are maddened (like King Pentheus).

What has happened to myself under the recent Neptune transits would not have been possible without what happened all those years earlier under the Pluto transits. They have been stages of unfoldment. During the height of what had become a Neptunian crisis for me in about 2015, I had a dream in which a woman, who was straightforward and had wisdom, told me that I was experiencing my second Psychosynthesis.

That is why earlier I likened these major transits to the Psychosynthesis model, in which a new element of the Self is wanting to emerge into consciousness, and in which there is often a crisis because we try to hang on to the old ways of being. When we get to the point that we are able to let go, then the crisis can resolve, and we can re-arrange ourselves around the new element that has come into consciousness.

When I was in my early 20s, I had a dream in which I was told that my name was 'he who has the ghost mind', because I was neither male nor female. On one level I was clearly male, and able to live as a male in a reasonably functional manner. What is seems to have been referring to, with the perspective of 40 years, was firstly the need for that deeper quality of independence, of the courage to trust my own judgement, that came with the Pluto transits of my thirties. This was my first Psychosynthesis, it was a new element that I had never imagined, that then changed my life completely. The second Psychosynthesis, to which the 2015 dream referred, was the entry of a feminine element, the absence of which was referred to in my early 20s dream. From around 2015, I was regularly having dreams about a woman I had forgotten about. Eventually, she descended into me, it was a very powerful experience, the pivotal experience of the series of Neptune transits that I had been experiencing. In a way, the transits were all leading up to this: the need to leave my relationship, to be on my own in a new way, to then 'cook' for a couple of years until I was ready for Sophia – as the Jungians call this archetype – to present herself, and change who I was. This Psychosynthesis was what the series of Neptune transits were leading up to. In this sense, these Neptune transits can be described as an 'ensoulment'. Particularly since Jung talks about the anima, the feminine, in the man being his soul (and the animus similarly for women – schematically, of course, it is never the same for everyone.)

When my Neptune transits were in their early stages in 2012, I was approached by a professional medium, who told me I needed to eventually leave the relationship I was in, or I would become ill. She had seen us together, and seen the disjunction of energies. I put up a fair bit of resistance over the next five years, but the push to leave was the strongest spirit-calling I have ever had, and eventually I just went with it. Neptune can be experienced as a calling, a longing from within to let our soul unfold, even though we may not know where that will take us, and the need to trust that calling sufficiently to act on it. That trust is something we can then take forward in life.

I did not get ill, but illness can play a significant role in these transits. My Pluto transits of the 90s did begin with illness. With what the doctor called 'post-viral fatigue', but that was just a medical term to make it sound like they knew something, which I don't think they did. I hadn't had a virus, and I had a strong sense that the depletion of my energy had a soul origin, rather than a purely physical origin. My natal Sun is in the 6th house in Aquarius, so major Sun transits are liable to affect my health (6th) and overall systems that connect (Aquarius).

This kind of hard-to-diagnose-and-treat illness is something we will probably encounter as astrologers, for they seem to be increasingly common, whether it is ME, fibromyalgia, irritable bowel syndrome, auto-immune diseases, allergies and many other syndromes. Astrology shows us that these illnesses are multi-level. Astrology concerns mind, body and soul as a whole, we are not split off in the way the conventional medical establishment often likes to see us. In my own case, I could see I was not going to get well until I listened to myself in a new way. Pluto had pulled the plug physically in order to get me to pay attention to my soul.

In the Shamanic cultures of the Far East, we find the 'Shamanic Illness', in which the spirits call a person to become a Shaman, and they will not recover, in fact they may well die, unless they respond to that call. And it seems to me that this is often a more suitable model for what is happening under these transits than is a medical diagnosis.

It is about calling, vocation. It is about the Self wanting to unfold further. It is about the spirits or the gods calling. Sometimes these illnesses can go on for years, because the change that is being asked for is big, it threatens our old sense of who we were. My own chronic fatigue took many years to overcome, it was incremental. The more I lived from that place of 'spirit', the more I trusted, and stopped trying to make things happen, the more whole and at ease I felt. But it was an old habit, and even now I can get the odd twinge, the sense of the plug being pulled, when I stop listening and operate from my head and will alone.

It can be a tricky area, because "soul ailment" easily translates into "psychosomatic" which translates into "it's all in your head and you are malingering." And then people can get into a terrible tangle trying to prove their illness is 'real', because there may not be a huge amount that is medically observable. Our task as astrologers is to go into the multi-level nature of these conditions without the client feeling we are denying the reality of the physical aspect. Sometimes people become identified with their illness, it becomes who they are, and that can be very tricky indeed for the astrologer to get near.

When Pluto or Neptune come calling, it is not just about a new level of Self that is trying to unfold. It is also about the defences that stand in the way of that, the personality we sometimes unconsciously construct as a child in order to cope, but which comes at the price of repression. These transits often ask us to come into relationship with this 'shadow' material. The other side of these illnesses is often unresolved trauma, that we have not felt ready to be with. That trauma can also be 'the crack where the light gets in'.

Chapter 6

Living with the Relational Self

As astrologers, we are helping people unfold who they are, and helping them to simply be with themselves. A therapist friend considers her primary job to be helping people 'tolerate' themselves. There is a lot in that. It is difficult, it can even contain hubris, to try to change ourselves. But we can at least stay with ourselves, and through that create space for change to happen.

The gods, the planets, are running this show, not us puny humans with our limited, one-sided perspective on everything. When I do readings, I liken the Sun and the Moon – the two main elements of our conscious personality – to the branches and roots of a tree. The Moon is the roots, and we can water and take care of them, but we can only ever know those roots that are near the surface. They go way down into the earth, as deep as you like, because we belong to the earth, we are nothing but her – and stardust, which is the same thing. The Moon is where we come from, and that is unknowable. Even our recent ancestors, who have shaped us profoundly, are largely a mystery to us, not to speak of the more distant past. But we remain a product of that long history.

In the same way that the Moon reaches down and back into the past, so does the Sun reach upwards and forwards into the future. It is the dynamic principle to the Moon's static principle. The Sun is who we are becoming, and that is also something we do not know. You get that sense sometimes of a bigger pattern behind your life, that it is unfolding to plan – even though you retain choice – and those are your branches growing upwards towards the Sun. All we can do is water the roots, take care of ourselves and run with those things that present themselves to us. But what we are becoming is a mystery.

The Venerable Bede tells the story of the missionary Bishop Paulinus who, in converting King Edwin of Northumberland, likened life to that of a sparrow which flies in through the door of the banqueting hall they were in, stays a short time, and flies out another door: we do not know where the sparrow has come from, or where it is going. Just so with our own short lives: we do not know where we have come from, or where we will go. Any knowing we have in this life is in the context of this greater not-knowing, this mystery that surrounds our life and even the fact that we exist. Anything we think we know has to be provisional.

So we are at the coalface, we are learning to tolerate ourselves, and we are hopefully helping our clients do that as they navigate their major transits. But we cannot 'change' ourselves, that is hubris. In the astrological context, it is only for the gods to know who it is that we are becoming. Our task is to learn to listen to them, and to distinguish their whispers from our own moods and prejudices.

In tolerating ourselves, we need to bring in the crucial element of not judging ourselves, of allowing whatever it is that is in our experience to simply be there. That way we become whole. The astrological chart is a map of wholeness. Imagine you are a piece of yourself cautiously poking its head into consciousness, and what you encounter is judgement, you get told you are 'bad', what are you going to do? You are going to run away, back into unconsciousness, where you are at least not being told you are the bad guy.

Judging ourselves is just more hubris, for how do we know what is good and bad, and what parts those pieces of ourselves, those planets, have to play? There is a scene in the *Lord of the Rings* in which Gandalf refuses to bemoan the detestable creature Gollum's existence, because he has a sense that Gollum has a part to play in the bigger scheme of things. Sure enough, right at the end, if it hadn't been for Gollum's obsession with the Ring, it wouldn't have been thrown into the Fires of Mount Doom, where it needed to go to save Middle Earth.

All these uncomfortable pieces of ourselves are planets. Our rage is Mars, our depression perhaps an undernourished Moon, our self-doubt an unrealised Sun, and so on. We all have these things, and we need to live with them, even love them. If you can use the chart to reflect someone back to themselves, and for them to start to accept and not judge who they are, then you have done a great job.

In earlier, indigenous societies, the self was relational, in the sense that who we are cannot be separated from our relationships with people and from the natural world around us. The modern, western self is more autonomous: it is seen as having its own separate existence, with its associated, and inalienable, rights and freedoms. The emphasis for a society with a relational self is on responsibilities and relationships. These are not absolute categories, for any society would partake of both. It is a question of emphasis. But it is one reason, for example, that the West finds it hard to understand China. For China, the self is more relational, in the sense that it is the collective good that matters most, rather than the rights of the individual. I am not trying to stand in judgement here, but rather trying to point out that what can seem to us like an unconscionable violation of the freedom of the individual may, in another context, appear rather differently.

I have a trust in indigenous ways, because their underlying principles are universal, and therefore seem to represent the way that is natural for humans to relate to the world. This might sound a bit intolerant of me in relation to the modern world view, but my position is pragmatic: living in balance is one of the emphases in all indigenous ways. Our modern way of seeing the world – with its more autonomous self, and its treatment of the natural world as a thing – has led to the greatest imbalance that has ever occurred. Therefore, it is not a worldview to live by, not as it is. I am open to any number of views if they work.

I am not so concerned with what is 'true': I take the view that everything is a story anyway, because ultimately all is the Great Mystery. And our modern stories need some serious reform. Astrology can find its place alongside many mythologies and stories, and we will look at this at more length later on.

For now, I am concerned with how we see the Self, and how that relates to astrology, and that will bring us back to how we can approach the shadow elements that usually surface under outer planet transits.

Nowadays we have the vision of wholeness as the goal of human life, and in this context the chart too becomes a vision of our wholeness, which is unique for each person. This is a vision that sits well with the idea of the Self as autonomous, and with Jung's idea of individuation.

However, I would suggest that the model of the Self that is natural to astrology is more relational. This seems blindingly obvious: after all, its starting point is that, at birth, the cosmos reflects who we are and the whole pattern of unfoldment that is to follow. This makes astrology fundamentally relational. I think that any ideas around wholeness that we bring in need to be seen, therefore, as useful but secondary. The goal of the relational self is not wholeness but living in balance with the world, as well as in balance within oneself. And that includes the planets/gods that are at the centre of the astrological paradigm.

The relational self does not see the planets as 'really' parts of our separate selves that have been projected onto the sky. No, those gods really are out there, they are awesome, we need to regularly remember them and make offerings to them. I have often had the experience of Pluto standing in the room as a guardian presence when I am writing about him.

The planet in the sky *is* the god or goddess. Symbols do not just stand for something; they *are* that thing. That can be hard for us to grasp from our intellectually sophisticated, materialist-scientific mindset. But it was natural to early peoples to think in this way.

Our fundamental perception as astrologers is through the fire element, through intuition. It is not the evidence of the senses, earth, and the theories consequent on that, air, through which we get our information. What we say needs to be corroborated by earth and air, but not in a narrow, one-sidedly scientific way.

The sky is full of these presences which we feel/intuit (feeling is the water element.) And they also describe who we are. Our being is not confined to this small physical body, it is spread out over the cosmos. We contain the whole Universe: this is one of Neptune's insights. The centre of who we are is also the centre of the Universe. And that makes us profoundly connected to all other forms of life, in which I include so-called 'inert' matter. We are the first society to see matter as dead, and for me that is enough evidence that we have got it wrong.

Chapter 7

Making Friends with the Spirits

We are a collection of presences/spirits/gods with a sense of 'I' as a provisional centre, that will dissolve at physical death. And this brings me back to the shadow work often catalysed by the major transits. An indigenous view is that these troublesome, even tormenting aspects of our life are not 'ours', they belong to the universe and are temporarily visiting us. We remain responsible for coming into a good relationship with them, but we do not need to identify with them. We do not need to label ourselves as an anxious person, or a depressive, or an alcoholic. They are spirits visiting us, and it is those spirits with which we need to come into relationship. This is a very strange, even fanciful point of view to take from the usual western perspective, but if we are astrologers, then we are already half way there. When you feel rage, it is Mars visiting you. Talk to him.

This idea is well-explained in *Healing the Soul Wound* by Eduardo Duran, who has Native American ancestry and works as a therapist with Native Americans, addressing the colonising of their minds by white ideas that has been going on for generations, and leaves them profoundly traumatised, and disconnected from who they are.

The language of spirits, the experience of them as real presences, is natural to indigenous people. Eduardo will say, for example, that you are being visited by the spirit of alcohol, which can be a medicine as well as a poison. Introduce yourself to this spirit, tell it who your parents and grandparents and other ancestors are, which is a traditional way. He will preface this by introducing some ceremony, burning some herbs and maybe calling on the powers of the four directions to be present and to help. This changes the whole context; it brings something into the room that awakens an ancestral memory in the Indian (as they call themselves). All this immediately changes the client's relationship with alcohol. Just a simple bit of ceremony and introducing himself to the spirit – and asking the spirit, in turn, to introduce itself.

So, hold those planetary gods and goddesses in mind, talk to them. It may be fairly straightforward, like Mars because you are raging, or Venus because you are having relationship difficulties. Or the Moon because you feel like you have a big hole inside of you. Or you may not know which god/goddess it is, so you can ask one to show up. Or it can be the planet doing the transiting that you need to talk to, or just have them with you. If you have a sense of Neptune around under one of his transits – which may go on for years – that can be a serious help. It doesn't mean there will be clarity – there is often a necessary unclarity as we move from one stage of who we are to the next. But you can feel supported and even inspired in the midst of a difficult situation.

These planets change the context of whatever we are going through. They make it so much bigger; they give a sense of profound significance. Life is always wanting to move on, that is its nature. The usual pattern seems to be that we have relatively short periods of intense change (though they can seem like they are going on forever) and longer periods of steady unfoldment, getting on with it, adding incrementally to the scales until we eventually tip over into some new period of change.

Chapter 8

Trusting in Death

These major transits help us to trust in life. We have the lone warrior archetype predominant in our society, fighting his way to the top, conquering nature. It is wilful, it is the masculine split off from the feminine, which offers a very different way of seeing life.

As I recounted in my own story, Pluto pulled the plug on my wilfulness when he squared my Sun in the early 90s, and I had to learn to listen in a different way. The following 30 years (to 2021) have been a process of listening and forgetting to listen, and then listening again, and all the time deepening my trust in the outer planets – in the Unconscious, in Spirit, in Life – that they have a design for my life, a series of unfoldments, and that my fundamental task is to co-operate with them, rather than run my life according to my own plans. How can you possibly plan your life in a long-term way if you are open to the intentions of the gods? We never know what they have in mind. I began writing this book shortly after writing my first book, on the Medicine Wheel. I had not seriously intended to write the first book, I was just vaguely thinking about it, until one morning I said to myself just do it, start writing, and see what happens. A book happened. I thought that was that, but then a few weeks later I realised I had an astrology book in me. That was a surprise too, and I just got on with it.

I could never have predicted any of the important developments in my life. But they keep happening, and the transits are a reliable guide to their nature and timing. Somehow, I never quite believe the transits until the events happen, and they always happen.

What all this has been slowly teaching me is to trust in the next stage of life. The gods have it in hand. They are onside with you, and only appear to be inimical if you want to carry on in the same old way. They can do what appear to be terrible things to facilitate, or even force, change. Ceres' daughter was abducted. People close to us may die. But the gods do not see that as a 'bad' thing, for death is something that is happening all the time. It is far more 'normal' to be dead than alive. Someone else's death may dismember us, but ultimately it frees us. Dying isn't so awful for the person who has died, it is the people left behind for whom it is difficult.

Pluto is death. Life is a series of Pluto-deaths. In the same way that life often slowly and painfully teaches us that we can trust whatever stage is coming next, so too does it teach us that we can trust death. For what else is death but the natural unfoldment of life into another stage?

In the mini-deaths that life provides, we are continually being flung into uncertainty and the unknown. Who are we without that spouse, without that career and its financial security, without the children at home, without the health we are used to relying on? Or without the looks and figure that got us noticed when we were younger: this is Pluto's helmet of invisibility, how do we value ourselves now?

Hopefully we get used to the insecurity and uncertainty that life keeps pushing our way. Indeed, we can come to relish it, it keeps life moving forward, it keeps it unfolding, it gives it a sense of voyaging into the unknown, which is thrilling, if we are prepared to take the risk. Would you want it any other way?

If we live according to that larger design, then I think we become more open, rather than more shut down, as we get older. I was wildly open when I was 20 years old, but very rigid and wilful in other ways. I have compromised my magic for long periods, but always claimed it back, renewed. And at the same time that rigidity has taken a hammering – I have learnt to trust, instead of 'making' things happen – so that I feel now – in my early 60s at the time of writing – at the start of the biggest adventure yet. Life has renewed itself in a way that I never expected, and I will say more about that when I talk about the second Saturn Return.

From this point of view, Death is the ultimate insecurity and uncertainty, but also therefore the greatest adventure. The trust we have gained through negotiating our major transits is also a training for death.

As the Indian poet Tagore said:

"And because I love this life, I know I shall love death as well."

By loving life, he did not mean chasing its pleasures: if that is all you do, then you will fear death, because it means the end of everything you want. No, he means that engagement with those deeper and demanding currents that flow through us all. Life is only truly fulfilling when we are living according to them, and rising with courage to what they ask of us. This is what the outer planets are really about.

Pluto will be standing there at our bedside when it is time to go, a benign presence giving us the courage to welcome the unknown; Neptune will be there, welcoming us back to the home we have forgotten, but which is deeply familiar. All the gods will be there, in one way or another. Jupiter too, orchestrating the occasion, welcoming us to the land of the gods.

As Pluto has been such a presence in my life – through his natal opposition to my Sun, and through the powerful dreams he has given me, through his 12ᵗʰ House placement – I hope to have a coin put in my mouth for the final journey, just as in ancient times coins were put in the mouths of the dead to pay the ferryman Charon, who took you across the river Styx into the land of the dead.

Chapter 9

The Real Qualification

These times of major change are also initiations into the Otherworld, the Spirit world, the world of the gods. It is this kind of deep initiation that I think is the real qualification to practise as an astrologer. I found my way in to astrology not through attending courses or by reading books or by talking to people, but by living through a series of Pluto transits in the 90s. Pluto dismembered me, eviscerated me, reduced me to rubble so that I could be rebuilt, with something otherworldly at my foundation. He took me off to his Underworld, and I was left with just enough energy to keep life going in this world, while I was off on my night-sea journey. And I came back with something strange, something other, that magic which is the foundation of being any kind of healer or counsellor or astrologer. Not the magic you get when you are young that sets you off on this path, but an integrated magic, that isn't just a part of you, but at the foundation of you. Incarnated magic (More on incarnation when we get to Saturn in Chapter 13.) You become like the ancient mariner, with his "long grey beard and glittering eye", who has had an awful initiation into life and death on a sea journey, and who feels compelled to tell his story to any who are capable of listening to it, who have something in them that can respond.

When we do an astrology reading for someone, yes, we are helping them to understand themselves. But it is coming from the gods, we are also initiating them into the Otherworld, we are giving them that context for understanding themselves. So how can we do that unless we have been deeply transformed by the Otherworld ourselves? Unless we have been sufficiently open when the gods came knocking at our door, to let them in and do their worst?

There is also this quote from Goethe:

"And so long as you haven't experienced this: to die and so to grow, you are only a troubled guest on the dark earth."

This is the real qualification to be an astrologer. You need to know the planets on your pulses, and that comes from letting them take you through a process of deep change. It is no different to the shaman in the far eastern cultures: the spirits come knocking, and she may get ill if she initially refuses their call. But eventually she has to yield, and that yielding is also a statement of the values you now live by: not the received values of the society around you, but what the Spirit, or the daimon, asks of you, which is a very individual matter. It is much harder to live in this way, because you do not have the easy sense of belonging and approval that comes from living according to the values of those around you. It takes a certain grit, a certain edge to live at that coalface. But it is the only place worth being, once you have been there. There is a satisfaction, a fulfilment that a life lived according to collective values can never give. The latter gives contentment, but the former brings joy.

Chapter 10

Astrology, Divination and Science

From this point of view, we are fortunate as astrologers that the presiding form of knowledge in our society is a scientific materialism that rejects astrology as nonsense. There is nothing that forces you to grow as a 'worthy opponent' does. We are forced to value astrology for ourselves, we have to live at that edge, from that connection in ourselves that knows the value of our calling. It is even better that that value cannot be expressed in 'scientific' terms, because then we do not have words and reason to fall back on, which can be a lazy form of knowledge. We have to stay with that visceral, or maybe heavenly, connection, which does not have adequate words. Real knowledge never does have adequate words, because words can only ever be descriptive pointers, they are not the thing itself, the experience itself. That is why science has its limitations: it is a partial and specialised form of knowledge.

So do not rail at the establishment's rejection of astrology, homeopathy and all the other intuitive ways of knowing and healing. Astrology is too subtle an art for many people to understand, however sharp their intellects may be. We are left alone to practise our craft, and there are no laws against it. We can be thankful for that. In the Middle Ages, we were proscribed by the church, because astrology was seen as conjuring up demons. In reality, it was a threat to the power of the church, which wanted a monopoly on access to the gods – or God, in their case.

It is much better to have a number of gods, as astrology does, where no one of them has the whole story. It is less likely to result in fundamentalism. Which doesn't mean that you don't get fundamentalist astrologers, who over-emphasise the 'correctness' of their tradition. But you will always find a certain amount of that, wherever you go.

I maintain that this opposition from establishment knowledge, from 'public reality', if you like, is good for us as astrologers. It forces us to go deeper into our own otherworldly connections, our own sense of vocation and its value. Protesting too much against the establishment shows, I think, that our personal foundations are not as solid as they might be. The astrologers on a mission to prove that astrology is 'scientific', and who retain a kind of faith that one day it will be shown to be such are, I think, a case in point. Astrology is not scientific, and that seems to me to be so obvious that a quest to make it so is not only quixotic, but also seems to suggest a need to look respectable, to be accepted by the establishment. And that misses the point of any vocation: it is literally a 'calling' from elsewhere, whose authority is not the received values of the collective.

I think there is an ongoing self-doubt amongst astrologers collectively because of the establishment scepticism. This is to be expected, because we are human. Let us acknowledge it, and not try to compensate for it by the awarding of too many prizes and degrees to each other. I am not saying they have no value, but there is a flavour to it, which I cannot prove, that sometimes suggests a compensation for self-doubt. Value the self-doubt, talk about it, honour it, for it is precisely our pathway to the gods. There will always be a certain amount of doubt around astrology, maybe we need at least one day a week where we think it is nonsense. That keeps us on our toes, it guards against complacency. The gods do not like it if we get too sure about what we are doing.

So, what is the relationship between astrology and science? Astrology uses the four elements of fire, earth, air and water respectively (that is the order in which they appear in the signs, beginning with Aries) as means of knowing and valuing. They are akin to Jung's four psychological functions of intuition, sensation, thinking and feeling, to a degree that Liz Greene suggests must have its origins in astrology. Jung, it seems, was much more of an astrologer than he let on, having his daughter draw up charts for all his clients.

Whereas we use all four elements, science emphasises just two of them, earth and air – data and theory. Fire and water, intuition and feeling, are seen as 'subjective' and downgraded accordingly. Fire, however, gives us the only real knowledge we can have. It comes to us from elsewhere and cannot be pinned down or proved. Ideas such as everything being conscious and connected to everything else, a sense of continuity of consciousness after physical death, the sense of the Great Mystery at the bottom of existence, are all fire. So is our ability to hit the nail on the head with a client.

If someone has, say, Mercury square Saturn, there are many things you could say about it. Our job is first of all to know all those things that could be said. But then to somehow, mysteriously choose those things that are accurate. Of course, our impression of the client gives us some clues, and in that way we 'cheat'. If they seem intellectually confident, for example, then that square has probably not disabled them. All the same, if we are experienced astrologers, we know that we come out with things that we could not have known. This has a powerful effect on the client.

A computer programme that interprets a chart does not have the fire element. It is purely mechanical, and therefore limited, in the way it operates. That said, there is the intuition of the programmer to be taken into account: the interpretations he or she gives to aspects may turn out to be appropriate for precisely those people who end up using the programme.

Geoffrey Cornelius makes a similar point about Sun Sign astrology in his book *The Moment of Astrology*. Sun Sign astrology is frequently ridiculed for being so general. How could the population possibly be divided into 12, and the things you write be true for that entire portion of the population? But it is not like that. Your prediction for the day for that sign will go in a particular newspaper, and be read by a certain number of people who bought that paper. Or looked on your website. If you are functioning intuitively, then the usual rules of space and time and what can and can't be known break down, and what you have written for, say, Aquarius, may apply precisely to those Aquarians who end up reading the column. This divinatory quality is at the heart of astrology, and it is a gift we can cultivate by honouring the gods and keeping them in mind.

It is also way outside of the remit of science. Science deals in repeatable events that can be analysed statistically. Astrology deals in individual events. Every act of divination is unique, every chart is unique, every person is unique.

At the same time, astrology does itself deal in generalities, but only up to a point. It may say, for example, that people with the Sun in Libra place more emphasis on relationship than most signs. It is a way in if you are doing a reading. In theory this could be tested scientifically, and *The Moment of Astrology*, Geoffrey Cornelius trawls through many of the studies that have attempted to verify, or disprove astrology in this way. After taking us through his meta-analysis, he says that the only reasonable conclusion is that astrology does not bear up to scientific analysis.

Sometimes there are results that have statistical significance, but there are many results that don't, and even the ones that are significant would almost certainly be hard to replicate. It is strange. There are certain things that as astrologers we know about various signs. But those things we know do not stand up to statistical analysis. We know there is truth to those things we think we know, not just because we have observed them, but because people find them helpful when we do readings. If you are doing a reading for an Aries, you can talk about their desire to always have some fresh vision in their life that they are moving towards, and this is by no means true for everyone.

Many people are happy to continue with things as they are. Or for a Pisces, it is a matter of 'not my will but thine', being guided in their lives by some bigger design, and not therefore needing to plan everything.

With our lists of the characteristics of each sign, we seem to have converted intuitive truth into rational, statistical truth. But if we push it too hard, if we try and pin it down with statistical analysis, it breaks down. There is a good contemplation as to the nature of reality when faced with this kind of situation.

In *Daimonic Reality* by Patrick Harpur, the author cites many accounts of fairy encounters going back centuries, along with modern accounts of UFOs, big black cats etc. There are too many of these, by reliable witnesses, to just dismiss them. Sometimes more than one person will see the same phenomenon. There was a sighting of a large alien spacecraft in Norfolk in the 70s. I know someone who saw it, and there were others who saw it too. In earlier times, groups of people would have the same vision of the Virgin Mary.

These experiences are real, but they cannot be pinned down. I know someone who saw one of the large black cats that are said to live in the UK countryside. He is a reliable witness. Yet no-one ever finds a dead black cat, and any photos of them are always ambiguous. Is that a moggy that just looks big because of the perspective?

The cumulative effect of reading *Daimonic Reality* is not just to persuade one of the actuality and widespread nature of these experiences – which don't tend to make it onto the news – but to inculcate a contemplation of the nature of reality itself. These experiences are just as real as anything else, but they are not literal.

We are a literal-minded culture, brainwashed into thinking that something is only real if it is tangible and can be measured. That is why after over 100 years, quantum physics has never really caught on in a mainstream kind of way. It is too subtle, and we want simple certainties to live by. Something is only real for us, in other words, if it can be described in terms of earth and air.

I think our lists of characteristics of the planets and signs, like fairies and big black cats, belong to daimonic reality: they are true, they are real; but they are not always true, or at least not in an obvious way; and if we try to pin them down by testing, they will move smartly out of the room. Like any self-respecting fairy would, subject to this kind of impertinence.

Astrology can find itself in the ridiculous position of having to justify its ways of knowing (fire/intuition) and valuing (water/feeling) via the specialised realms of earth and air. It is, of course, not possible.

The true position is that astrology belongs to a broader and more inclusive tradition of knowledge than does Science, because it uses all four elements, and science uses just two. It is impertinent of science to stand in judgement over astrology. Science is the specialisation, the junior partner that provides certain kinds of information, but does not address the full range of human experience and knowledge, as astrology does. I think it is unfortunate, albeit understandable, that some astrologers feel they need a 'scientific' justification for their art. We need, if anything, to be on the offensive, reminding science of its subsidiary place and the limitations of its methods.

This is Stephen Fry, an English light entertainer and cultural spokesman, on the subject of astrology:

"All astrology is absolutely and without reservation the bullest of bullsh*t that ever there was. It is a senseless delusion that does not even have the benefit of being harmless fun. It is a harmful bore. Harmful to the human spirit, harmful to the dignity and wonder of the real universe and the real power of the mind to think for itself. I hate astrology with a fervor that is almost frightening."

Is this essentially any different to the medieval mindset that saw as heresy any knowledge that was not in accord with the Church's interpretation of the Bible? Fry reveals an intolerant, fundamentalist mindset behind his liberal-spokesman front. His vehement opposition not just to astrology but to religion too is interesting, given that he suffers from manic-depression – now called 'bi-polar' – and has tried to kill himself a number of times. He presents himself as a high priest of rationality, and it is as if in opposing astrology and religion, he is trying to keep at bay the non-rationality in himself. He may find himself screaming for a priest on his deathbed! As may Professor Richard Dawkins, another evangelical atheist.

If asked to justify astrology, I think it is more real, truer to the actual context to point out the limitations of the scientific method, which is purely concerned with what it calls 'objective' reality (which is an illusion), while conveniently ignoring the biggest reality of all, which is the 'subjective'. For in the last analysis, that is what everything comes back to: personal experience, which includes what we might call the transpersonal, or the outer planets.

However, unless the situation really calls for it, I would prefer to sidestep and introduce the concept of 'Two Eyed Seeing', a term created in 2004 by Mi'kmaw Elder Albert Marshall.

> *"It refers to learning to see from one eye with the strengths of Indigenous knowledges and ways of knowing, and from the other eye with the strengths of Western knowledges and ways of knowing ... and learning to use both these eyes together, for the benefit of all."*
> (http://www.integrativescience.ca/Principles/TwoEyedSeeing/)

In the philosophy of science, it comes under the heading 'Explanatory Pluralism'.

It is an essentially pragmatic philosophy. As modern westerners, our instinct is often to burrow away at different theories, until we have proved one of them right, and the other wrong. All that really matters, however, is that the practice which comes out of the theory works, that it gets good results.

"If it's real, it works. If it works, it's real,"

according to Jim Tree, Native American author of *The Way of the Sacred Pipe*, astrology works, we know this. And homeopathy. And acupuncture. But they are not very amenable to being proved scientifically. Science says that something is only true if it can be proved to be so on its own very particular terms, using repeatability, statistics and theory. This is not unreasonable within certain parameters, but the world got along very well without these parameters for millennia.

Two-Eyed Seeing is partly a corrective to this tendency of science towards fundamentalism, towards wanting everything to be true and valid purely on its own terms. And how can that ever be? Theories are only descriptions of reality, they are not reality itself, which is unknowable. More than that, Two-Eyed Seeing is asking that conventional and alternative medicines and other forms of knowledge leave each other alone and stop criticising each other; rather, they need to respect and appreciate each other.

This intolerance goes both ways. We have probably all seen how conventional medicine can be so dismissive and antagonistic towards disciplines such as homeopathy. But people on the 'alternative' side can be just as dismissive and disrespectful of conventional medicine. Vaccination, for example, is one of the better things that conventional medicine does. It is using a small amount of like-for-like to catalyse the body into marshalling its own defences against disease. The science is pretty solid. And yet it gets attacked, using pseudo-science that makes very little sense. Such attacks make their proponents look ignorant and prejudiced. Now there is nothing wrong with having an alternative to vaccine, using, for example, homeopathy. That is laudable. But it is not either/or. If your alternative approach has to be 'right' and conventional medicine 'wrong', then you are participating in the same rigid, fundamentalist mindset that caused the problems in the first place.

It is liberating to be able to hold two different ways of seeing the world at once. It is what the poet Keats called 'negative capability', the ability to hold in our mind's contradictory stories about how the universe is "without any irritable reaching after fact and reason". It changes the way we see the whole of life. It grounds us more in experience and less in ideas. And it shows us the real nature of the mind. It is not there to create rigid theories to explain and justify our life (though it can certainly be used like that.) The mind used rightly is a servant that holds a number of different and useful explanations of reality, but all they are is explanations, and their multiplicity reveals the abundance and variety of life itself, if we allow ourselves into its flow. Achieving this, however, is more than a mental exercise: we tend to be one-sided about everything, for emotional reasons.

Astrology is one explanation for how things work, and science is another. Neither has to be explicable in terms of the other. They are both, in the last analysis, useful stories about how things are, and why should one story be reducible to the other?

Chapter 11

The Elemental Balance

At the start of this book, I spoke about the value of simple astrology, in that it keeps us close to the symbols, and that is where the power of astrology as a divinatory tool comes from. It is difficult for the gods to speak through us if we are not feeling them. We are now returning to this theme of simple astrology through considering the four elements of fire, earth, air and water. This, if you like, is even more experiential than a consideration of the Sun and Moon, for the elements are right with us, all the time. They are what we are made up of. We are nothing apart from them. Sun, soil, wind and rain, you can probably feel them as I say them.

Astrology easily becomes quite intellectual and disconnected from physical experience. Yet it is through the body that the gods speak. In medieval churches, the congregation used to dance, along with the priest. In that way, people made their own ecstatic connection with the Divine. So, course it was banned, and pews were introduced so that people could not dance (See *Dancing in the Streets: A History of Collective Joy* by Barbara Ehrenreich). If people are making their own connections with the Divine, then their source of authority lies within themselves, rather than with the priest, and upwards through the hierarchy. And if the hierarchy no longer has the authority, then the people can no longer be controlled. So, if you not only ban dancing, but declare the body and its pleasures to be the work of the Devil, then you keep control. This is how religions work. One way or the other, divine authority has to rest with the hierarchy rather than with the people. And it is not really the evil hierarchy 'doing' this to people: it is a collective and unconscious contract, because not many people want their freedom in this way, it does not have the security and certainty they crave. It is the collective itself that sets up these disempowering hierarchies, rather than a few evil people who have managed to seize control against the will of the people. We are, however, ambivalent about both our freedom and our servitude, so we rail against our 'captors', while secretly enjoying the security they provide. This goes a long way to describing many people's attitude to government (which is not nearly as powerful as we think it to be.) As Dr Johnson said:

"How small, of all that human hearts endure, that part which laws or kings can cause or cure."

I am, however, starting to digress. My point is that we have been brainwashed into downgrading the earth element, firstly by the Christian church, and latterly by science, with its separation of mind and body. Instead of being the work of the devil, the body is now 'dead' matter. I'm not sure which is worse, but in neither case is the body the vehicle for the divine, which is part of its real nature. We have seen a natural reclaiming of the body's potential for ecstasy in recent decades through, for example, rock'n'roll music, raves, and Pentecostal churches.

So not only is it helpful as an astrologer to stay connected with the sky, it is also helpful to feel connected to this planet. And to start to overcome that separation from nature – and from the feminine – which has been going on for so long in our culture.

I say this as a pre-amble to a consideration of the elemental balance within the chart, that can give us much very basic information about ourselves. I look at in a two-fold way: the planets in their signs tell us something about the elements that do or don't come naturally to us; the planets in the houses tell us which elements we are driven to embody, to incarnate.

The elements begin with our felt experience of them: of sun, soil, wind and rain. One level of abstraction on, and we can think of them as the psychological functions as described by Jung: intuition, sensation, thinking and feeling respectively.

I prefer just to use the inner planets when considering the elements. This is because they concern the type of person we consciously feel ourselves to be, whereas the outer planets come from somewhere else, they are not part of this little earth vehicle we are trying to live in, but rather concern the larger designs that the gods have for us. This is, however, just my personal preference. I'm never entirely sure whether to include the Angles in the elemental balance of who we are, because they are house cusps, but on the other hand they are so close to us – particularly the Asc – that they may as well be part of who we are.

So, the elemental balance is not an exact art, but it can give a few useful, broad brushstrokes. In my own case, I have three planets in air, two in fire, one (plus Asc) in earth and one in water. It is a reasonably balanced distribution, apart from water. And that is about right: I function strongly through imagination and vision and ideas (fire and air) and those ideas need to be practical, they need to relate to experience (as you might have noticed in this book), which is earth. It has always been water that has been difficult for me: knowing what I am feeling, and trusting it enough to act from it. I would say that it wasn't until my mid-fifties that I started to become confident that I had an adequate grasp of what I was feeling. These things can take time.

If I look at the elemental balance by house, there are two in fire, one in earth, one in air and three in water. So there it is! I was born with a shortage of the water element, but life has required that I find it and live it. We saw this earlier, when I talked about the transit of Pluto to my Sun in the 90s: my life had got to the point where it was no longer going to work unless I began to pay attention to feeling, and less to ideas of what I 'should' be doing.

Life may not have asked this of me. There is no inherent requirement that we become equally functioning through all the elements, it may easily not be who we are. We just need an adequate functionality within each element in order to live our lives. For some people, it may mean, for example, that they become just about grounded enough to keep a roof over their heads while they compose music, or paint.

The four elements are in one sense 'equal', and needing some kind of balancing. In another sense, they are a cumulative journey from fire through to earth then air and then water. The Medicine Wheel I use describes this journey (with pretty much the same elemental meanings) as fire then water then earth then air. The ordering is quite different, which shows that we need not to hold these things too rigidly.

But the astrological journey is fire, earth, air, water. Aries, Taurus, Gemini, Cancer. Then we begin again with Leo, and so on. It is the same with the houses. We of course inhabit all the houses, the various spheres of life, to some extent at different times.

Some astrological systems also describe life as a slow journey through the houses, for about six years each, beginning with the 1st house, and taking it from there. From this point of view, we can see life as a journey of incarnating the elements, with the emphasis on different elements at different ages.

I'm not so inclined to divide life up in this way, because an emphasis on any element can occur at any age. It's a bit too schematic for my taste. That said – and this is my own preference – I think we can broadly divide life into four great stages of say 20 years each, corresponding to the elemental journey, providing we allow room for sub-themes within each of those stages. We begin with fire, the first creative spark of new life. This is the early part of life, when everything is new. Then we reach adulthood, and the need to create a material existence for ourselves, and that is earth. After many years consumed by the demands of that journey – which usually means career, marriage and children – it starts to come to an end, our perspective starts to shift away from collective to individual values, and this is the mid-life passage, or crisis. Air is that ability to stand back and weigh up options, instead of being compelled by ambition, biology, societal expectations, childhood woundings etc. So, there is some wisdom that begins to come in with air. It is where life begins to contemplate itself, having some experience with which to do so.

The perspective of air is a cognitive quality: it has truth, but it is limited, it is not a quality of our whole being. We have not merged with those truths. Take death: it is an air quality to know that we are going to die, and that we may as well accept it, because it's going to happen anyway. But that doesn't mean we are not afraid of it. We haven't necessarily found what you might call the emotional equivalent of our cognitive awareness.

This leads into the 4th great stage of life, which is water, or feeling. Life has gradually made its way through from its initial spark into matter, then to contemplation of itself, and finally into a merging with those truths it has discovered. In the case of death, there is a full acceptance of it once we reach water, based on the insight that life is essentially no different to death, they are both part of the same thing. We know these things 'in our waters'.

Astrology gives us guides from the sky to help steer our lives, but the essential journey we are undertaking is through these four elements, from fire to earth to air then to water, over and over, until we have become them. And a strong relationship with those elements as we experience them within the natural world will deepen our engagement with that journey.

Initiation, Incarnation, Perspective and Integration. These are four key words we can use respectively to describe the aspect of life that we are attempting to live within each element.

Chapter 12

Tweaking Our Creation Mythologies

The three outer planets – Uranus, Neptune and Pluto – cannot be seen with the naked eye, which is why they were not discovered until recent times. Not being visible, they are not part of our conscious endowment, unlike the inner planets: they are not here to be 'mastered' (as much as a god or goddess can ever be 'mastered'.) They come from somewhere much bigger, rawer and more primordial. They describe collective consciousness and its currents, and the way that works through us on an individual level.

They also make a great mythological add-on to one of our modern creation mythologies, namely the Big Bang (the other one being Evolution.) My reservation about the Big Bang story is that it gives no magical or miraculous origins to the universe. It is probably the first creation myth ever to do this, which means either we have become super-evolved and seen through the superstitions of 'primitive' people, or we have forgotten something very important. I tend to side with the latter interpretation.

The psyche is an objective reality (as Jung pointed out) every bit as much as the material reality around us, and the psyche needs magic in its stories of how we came to be. If there is no magic in our creation stories, where did the magic in us come from?

As has been pointed out, the Big Bang describes a process of everything suddenly arising from nothing, and if that is a not a miracle, then what is? But anyway, let us suppose that to start with there is nothing. Apart from the gods, who exist outside of time and space, they have 'always' been there. And Uranus, who is the creative spark, says "Hey guys, I've had this great idea for a thing called a universe" and without so much as a by-your-leave he lights the blue touch paper. At that point Pluto steps in, with his capacity to contain tremendous power within a tiny seed, and a huge expansion begins. As it does so, the primordial imagination of Neptune is activated, and the universe is given form and beauty in the shape of particles and atoms and light, in an evolving dance that gradually produces nebulae and stars and planets that continue to dance around each other. This was the way in which the gods – or the archetypal powers, existing outside of time and space – created the universe.

I don't see this creation story as a fanciful overlay to what 'really' happened. It was an event, according to science, that occurred some 14 billion years ago. No-one was around to see it. We believe in it purely because certain arcane squiggles balance each other – by which I am referring to the mathematical equations of physics. This doesn't mean it is not true. But as mentioned earlier, science only ever models aspects of reality, it is not reality itself. Any thoughtful scientist would tell you this. Science is therefore stories – models – about life and the universe.

We have the brainwashing of 'facticity' to contend with in the way science usually presents itself: namely, that science tells us what is actually the case, and the rest is 'just' stories. But would it have been any different in the Middle Ages? People took the Bible literally, and believed as fact its account of how God created the world. The rest was heresy.

I once asked a Chippewa Cree teacher if his people became fundamentalist about their Creation Myth, and he said no, because they have more than one such myth, and they contradict each other. He also viewed evolution as a story.

Science can be just as fundamentalist as Christianity ever was, fundamentalism being the idea that there is only one reality. As astrologers, we know this is not the case. There are the ten different realities of the ten gods/planets for starters. I am sure those gods would object strongly if we tried to explain any of them in terms of the other ones.

Besides all this, our origins and destiny are deeply mysterious things anyway, as I recounted earlier in the story of Bishop Paulinus and the sparrow. Indigenous peoples have their creation stories and their explanations of how things are, and many people will take them fairly literally, because that is how people often are and always have been: they need a fairly simple set of beliefs about how things are, and just want to get on with their lives on that basis. But the elders, the people with some serious wisdom, know that really everything is the Great Mystery.

It is the same with science: it provides some fairly simple ideas about the nature of the universe, much as medieval Christianity did in its own way, and for many people that is good enough. The universe began with the Big Bang, life has arisen through a process of evolution, when we die there is extinction, and the universe will end with a whimper at some unimaginably distant point in the future. The nature of life and the universe is, from this point of view, very straightforward and maybe, to many, self-evident.

It is to be expected that many will take science literally and simply, in a way that leaves no room for something like astrology. Many people, maybe most people, want to know what is what, and what is right and wrong, and always have done. And they want to be told these things by a reputable collective authority. They may well have an unhelpful psychological breakdown if you were to take their pillars of certainty away from them. This is another reason for not getting too upset when people dismiss astrology.

As I said near the start of this book, quantum physics showed over 100 years ago that consciousness, rather than matter, is primary. As Max Planck, the originator of quantum theory, said,

"I regard consciousness as fundamental. I regard matter as derivative from consciousness. We cannot get behind consciousness.

Everything that we talk about, everything that we regard as existing, postulates consciousness."

Our everyday reality is dreamed into being, on an ongoing basis. But that is hard to pin down for people who want to know what-is-what. So it is unlikely to catch on.

It does mean, however, that the gods are dreamed into being. Mercury, Venus, Jupiter and the rest of them, as gods and goddesses, are dreamed into being. Dreamed by what is a mystery. But that does not mean they are not real. Neil Gaiman's fantasy novel, *American Gods* is a story of how the Old World gods came over to America with the early settlers, but are now dying out because not many people believe in them anymore. Instead, they believe in the new gods such as Mr World and Mr Town and Media. Central to the story is Odin, who is trying to rally the old gods to take on the new.

The point is that the gods need to be believed in to continue to exist. That doesn't make them 'just' beliefs, however. When we believe in something, we dream it into being. The poet William Blake said that

"Imagination is the real and eternal world of which this vegetable universe is but a faint shadow."

Asked

"When the sun rises, do you not see a round disc of fire somewhat like a guinea?"

he replied,

"O no, no, I see an innumerable company of the heavenly host crying Holy, Holy, Holy is the Lord God Almighty."

Reality and the human imagination cannot be separated. I want to emphasise at this point that just because I have some reservations about the epistemological claims of science, does not make me a science-basher. Many people think in the two categories of for or against. I find science very interesting, and I think it has done some great things and continues to do so. My main point is that it provides us with useful stories, 'modelling', not facts. When we think it provides facts, then it becomes a belief system, which is what it has largely become. As long as it is seen as a set of stories alongside other ones of equal status, then I do not have a problem with it. More than that, I value it.

Because science is a set of stories, it has been dreamed into being. And it can be re-dreamed. Which is what I was doing when I told the story of the presence of Uranus, Neptune and Pluto at the beginning of the current universe. These dreams come from somewhere bigger than ourselves, they are not just whims.

Jupiter is the planet of story-telling. But I think that Neptune, the planet of the Imagination, is the ocean out of which the stories are picked. Neptune is that place where consciousness and matter merge, where it becomes obvious that you cannot separate human consciousness and the universe that consciousness is always trying to understand and describe.

Evolution is our other modern Creation Myth. Behind it is not just the idea of life as a process of continual unfoldment and renewal, but a mechanism for it (rather a brutal one), along with the suggestion that what comes later is 'better', more advanced, than what came before. It is an idea that has seeped into astrology, with the idea of 'evolutionary astrology', which is why I want to discuss it.

At Forrestastrology.com, Steven Forrest and Jeffrey Wolf Green lay out a series of principles which they see as fundamental to evolutionary astrology. The idea that the soul is in a process of 'evolution' over a series of lifetimes is taken as a starting point, with the birth chart describing our point in that evolution, at the beginning of our current incarnation.

My basic problem with this idea is that astrology is cyclical, rather than linear. Evolution is a linear idea, in which you go from A to B. This is not how early people thought. For them, the purpose of living was to do so in a balanced way, in balance with the gods, and in balance with the natural world. End of story. It is entirely experiential, in that if we live in a balanced way, then life goes well. And if it is not going well, then we need to look to see where we are unbalanced. To posit a direction of unfoldment over lifetimes is an intrusion into the Great Mystery of existence of the idea of the autonomous self with a linear trajectory. It is an abstraction, which we moderns are very prone to. It is fundamentally a religious belief, that seems to be provided without evidence.

Astrologers are story-tellers. That is what we do when we give someone an astrology reading: we are giving people useful stories about themselves, that are also true, because the gods have spoken them. But these stories dance between literal and metaphorical truth.

As a story teller, an evolutionary astrologer could no doubt look at your South Node – past lives – and tell you a beautiful story about where you have come from, that explains much in your present life. And then look at your North Node – where you are headed, what you are here to learn – and tell you an inspiring story about that too, that is also useful. I would say fine, but don't take it too literally. I find my own South and North Nodes describe very well the past conditioning and ongoing learning of my present life. I don't need to invoke past or future lives. Keep it simple, keep with what you can know. Stories about our past lives can be very seductive. It seems very easy, for example, to persuade people that they were burnt as witches in past lives, which can then be used to explain much of their current experience, but how true those stories are, and how useful they are, is another matter.

The self is an illusion; if we look for it, we cannot find it (this is basic to Buddhist practice), and part of becoming balanced is to align ourselves with what is real rather than with our illusions. If the self is notional, then there is every chance it will evaporate at death. The self is a convenient falsehood that we need to live by. It is foolish to become attached to it and give it metaphysical status. That does not make death an extinction. Life almost certainly goes on. There is too much evidence of this for any reasonable person to deny. But in a way that is beyond our ken.

I think it is far truer to our experience to remain agnostic about what happens before and after death: this is not a blankness, but a fullness, for that sense of the mystery that pervades everything has more room to enfold us.

Evolution gets treated as another scientific fact, it is what 'really' happened, and if you have your reservations, then that makes you a benighted creationist. Humanity so often loves to think in two categories, one right and the other wrong. Either you accept all the findings of climate science, for example, or you are a climate denier. What I will say for creationism is that at least it gives a miraculous origin to life.

Evolution is a good story, provided we can leave room for other stories, and take the judgement out of it, in the sense of assuming that what came after is 'better' than what came before. Because modern people don't usually think mythologically, it can be hard for them to spot that the Idea of evolution is an inversion of the medieval Great Chain of Being. In the latter mythology, you have God at the top, then angels and demons, then men, women, animals, plants and rocks and stones. Evolution starts at the other end, at the bottom: out of 'inanimate' matter arose the first life forms, which gradually worked their way upwards until at the top you find not God, but Man, in our glorious hubris.

Evolution not only flatters humans as being 'better' than

other life forms, it also, through its mechanism of 'survival of the fittest', i.e., law of the jungle, reflects the ethos of the Victorian Capitalism of the time when the theory was first promulgated. Another society, it might be argued, might have hit on 'co-operation' as the fundamental driving force: why not, when we see such complex and balanced systems of different life forms arising naturally? Maybe the creation of new types of beauty is the fundamental driver? This fits far better with a dream I once had, in which I saw a speckled moth that was closely blended to its surroundings, and in which I was given to understand that the theory of evolution only explains a very thin slice of how this situation came to be.

As for the evidence for evolution, as a science it gets away with a sparse amount that no other science, apart from the pharmaceutical industry (which has little idea of how its drugs actually work), would get away with. But that is because evolution has become a religious idea, a belief.

I am not trying to trash evolution, because it is a good story in some respects. But it has its limitations. A useful book in this respect is *Shattering the Myths of Darwinism: A rational criticism of evolution theory* by Richard Milton. This is a difficult area, because so many people have got hold of the idea of evolution as a solid fact, and hold it with fervour, such that you become suspect, irrational if you attempt to question it.

Not only does evolutionary astrology attempt to impose within a linear framework what is a cyclical mythology, but some astrologers attempt to place humanity collectively within this type of thinking. If you have done much mundane astrology, in which the charts of countries are considered, along with the transits that impact on them, it quickly becomes clear that it is a merely human judgement to insist that the change for the country consequent upon a transit is 'better' or one step further on in its process of 'evolution'. All we can do is to describe the changes that have occurred.

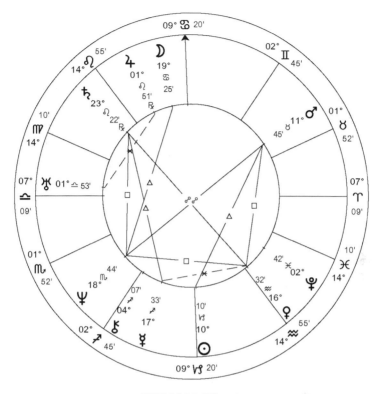

UK 1801 Chart

The UK was at the end of series of hard Pluto transits to its Angles, Sun and Moon when the EU referendum occurred in 2016. When a transit is part of a series, the change it is ushering in may not be apparent until the whole series is complete, as though it is all growing underground for years in advance before it is ready to push above the soil. In the case of the referendum, it seemed likely to me from an astrological viewpoint that the UK would vote to leave, because how else to explain the major change that was upon the UK? The astrology in many ways described well what happened, particularly the final transit, which was Pluto opposite the Moon: the people (the Moon) claiming their power (as they saw it) back from the EU.

So the UK left the EU. But was it an 'evolution' for the country? That seems like a human judgement to me, that may or may not have a point, but it has nothing to do with the astrology, which merely described what happened. I am sure that no Remainer (which I assume includes the majority of my British readers) would see it as an 'evolution', and this is therefore a good example for such readers as to why astrology is not 'evolutionary'. It is just one cycle leading into another cycle, as the planets revolve endlessly around the earth.

Not only is it problematic to make evolutionary judgements about countries, but by the same token it is problematic to judge in this way about humanity generally. We simply roll on from one phase to another. I think the idea that we are collectively 'evolving' is part of the scientific/imperialist hubris that we have inherited from the past, in which early peoples were seen as 'primitive'.

My experience of indigenous people who are living from their traditions is not one of 'primitiveness', but of a rounded humanity, and a sophistication of thought which we, with our black and white categories, are rarely capable of. To talk about a collective 'evolution' against this backdrop seems absurd.

In *The Passion of the Western Mind*, astrologer Richard Tarnas says that it has been the task of masculine consciousness to forge its own autonomy and then come to terms with the great feminine principle in life, and thus recover its connection with the whole. This will constitute

"the fulfillment of the underlying goal of Western intellectual and spiritual evolution." (p442)

In *The Philosopher's Secret Fire (pp 263-6)*, Patrick Harpur takes issue with this position:

"Evolution is a spirit notion which soul does not recognise. Traditional societies do not evolve. They live within a mythology which contains all imaginative possibilities, Earth Goddesses no

less than Heraclean egos... Because we are changing, we think of ourselves as evolving. We are not. We are literalising the old myths... If the rational ego is to disappear it is more likely to be destroyed by the ricochets of ideologies made in its own image."

There is a superstition that it is only modern people who have a developed sense of a distinct individuality, along with the 'objective' rationality that comes with that. My experience is that indigenous people have the sense of collective consciousness and connectedness that we have lost, and which we have become suspicious of; but if you speak to any elder, you will soon find they are not lacking in distinct individuality and rationality either.

Maybe there is some larger design behind the way the masculine has become split off from the feminine, and by the same token from nature, in the modern world. Or maybe there isn't a larger design. Maybe it is just what has happened. There are limits to what we humans, with our tiny slices of consciousness compared to the vast consciousness of the cosmos, can know (this is a traditional indigenous idea.) But I think it is best not to make the disastrous split in western consciousness 'right' by assuming an evolutionary purpose to it. All we can say is that it has happened, and do what we can to heal that divide. As the poet Ted Hughes said:

"The story of mind exiled from Nature is the story of Western Man."

In that place of honest unknowing, I think there is more room for the gods to speak. Besides, when did humanity, particularly in its vast modern collectives, ever learn anything for more than about five minutes? It doesn't seem to work that way.

So, we have the Big Bang and Evolution bringing the Universe and Life into being respectively. There is also an End Times to our modern Creation Mythology: instead of Armageddon, we have Heat Death. This idea arises out of the Second Law of Thermodynamics, which says that the amount of disorder (entropy) in a system always increases over time. This means that the Universe as a whole is gradually running down: it is gradually becoming more dispersed and less ordered. The eventual result of this, billions of years down the line, is that the universe will be so dispersed that there will be nothing, no energy, there at all. And this is called Heat Death.

Can we introduce magic into this grey nothingness? There is a way in which I view scientific theories, and the evidence for them, as the universe corresponding to the way we imagine it. If you have imagined the Higgs Boson, and you go looking for it, sooner or later there is a good chance you will find it. That does not make it 'imaginary'. It is real. But consciousness and matter inform each other. So, I think the idea of Heat Death reflects our modern demonisation of the universe: we have already decided the universe is essentially dead and indifferent to us (what a contrast to the indigenous idea that Mother Earth is alive and takes care of us), and Heat Death just seems to be a corollary of that. It is a denial of the reality of Spirit and the Imagination.

Maybe Heat Death is salvageable in the sense that we can tweak it to make it imaginatively satisfying. But what I want to do is to put in a counter-notion. Is your experience of the world that it is gradually running down? If we leave out the actions of modern humanity for a moment, surely our experience of the natural world is that it is continually renewing itself? That it does so is one of the wonders and beauties of life. Moreover, there are indigenous people who ceremonially greet the Sun every day, with the idea that if they did not express gratitude to the Sun in this way, it would cease to rise. Putting this together, the continued renewal of the world and the life within it, is dependent upon our appreciation of it. That is why it is good to leave offerings to the natural world and to the various beings, seen and unseen, which inhabit her. If we do not relate to the natural world with an attitude of appreciation, but one of exploitation, then she will gradually die – she will suffer from 'entropy'. That is why it is said that the fairies are disappearing: because we forget to remember them nowadays (I try to leave them offerings myself at places where I feel they are present.) Science and an attitude of treating the world as a 'thing' to be exploited often go together (they don't have to), so the idea of entropy is a natural consequence. The way the psyche understands this theory is that everything is gradually getting worse. But it doesn't have to be like this. Make offerings to the natural world to avoid Heat Death! Modern science has its 'laws' of physics. But who says they do not change over time, that they have to remain the same? Personally, I take it quite literally that if we were all to feed and appreciate the natural world, then she would not be slowly running down as alleged. As astrologers, making offerings to the natural world, expressing our thanks to the Sun for giving us life, will not only help the universe, it will make us better astrologers.

To conclude this section, one of the main points I am wanting us to come away with is the idea that astrology is about cycles rather than linear directions, and that is the way humanity has always perceived life until recently. The purpose of our lives is not to engage in some imagined unfoldment taking place over lifetimes, but to live in balance with nature and with the gods while we are here. This is something we can experience and verify for ourselves, whereas the unfoldment over lifetimes, while an appealing idea, is largely a supposition, and it maybe gives a sense of continuity and importance to the modern autonomous self that it does not in reality have.

Chapter 13

Saturn

Saturn is the worldly taskmaster, at least in the earlier stages of our life. He is the outermost of the visible planets, and therefore rules the boundaries, structures and laws within which the rest of life takes place. He tells us to incarnate. Like Pluto, his message is that life is not about ascension to higher spheres of existence, but of arriving here on the planet, viscerally and corporeally, embodying the spirit that courses through us. When we are around 29 years old, he spends a year re-visiting the place he was in the sky when we were born. And his message is that it is time to shift our emphasis from the explorations of youth to the responsibilities of adulthood.

You can see this like clockwork in the charts of people when they are close to that age: they get a promotion at work, they buy their first house, or get married, or have their first child. It is generally some new and enduring worldly responsibility that comes into their lives, and is part of the process of incarnation. Saturn's lessons are often difficult too, which is why he has a bit of a bad name. But they are only difficult because when we are younger, the qualities he asks of us – patience, responsibility, mastery, discipline – often have to be learned.

We would maybe rather continue to play, and the importance of play at all ages is not to be underestimated, it is the spirit of play that keeps us young and able to keep renewing ourselves. That, however, is the *Puer* (or *Puella*) *Aeternus*, the Eternal Youth, which exists in a dialectic with the *Senex*, the Old Man, or Saturn. Schematically, the visionary *Puer* has had a good run for 28 years or so, and it is time for the *Senex* to have his say.

At the Saturn Return, it is as if we have spent our twenties exploring and discovering different threads within ourselves, and the time comes to pull them all together and make something of them. It is the time of "Don't tell me about your visions unless they grow corn."

Saturn is not just worldly responsibility. He is also the responsibility to that deeper thing within us which needs to live, to become more whole. So sometimes the Saturn Return will be the other way round: someone may have spent their earlier years trying to do the conventional thing, building a career etc, and Saturn comes along and says that's not for you any more, there is something else in you to which you need to pay attention. It is Saturn as vocation.

Saturn can easily become one-sided. He can say that only that which can be observed and measured is of value. In this way he becomes a denier of, instead of the servant to, the outer planets, for which his role is to be a bridge, to help give them form on this earthly plane.

This one-sidedness becomes a theme when there are challenging aspects to Saturn in the birth chart. These aspects may on the one hand mean that we are reluctant to incarnate, because we don't want to get our hands dirty, that we are afraid that we will lose our magic if we 'sell our souls' to Mammon, as it can seem. This is the projection of demonic qualities onto the world that is very common amongst spiritual bypassers. The world is ruled by evil people, as they see it, not necessarily ones that they can name, but they are the people responsible for all the bad things in the world, and they need to be opposed.

I saw a picture taken at an Extinction Rebellion protest, in which a young man had a placard blaming CEO's, oil companies, politicians and sundry others for the state of the planet, and which side were we going to choose? It presumably had not occurred to him that, for example, the oil companies only exist because we all use petrol. It needs to be 'us and us', not 'us and them'. This is a typical example of the denial of Saturn. It is not productive, because once you have made someone the enemy, they are going to push back, and the result is polarisation rather than progress. This does not mean that the protesters do not have a point, of course they do, but it gets compromised by this projection of Saturn.

You can see the same dynamic in many protest movements. It is sometimes there in Feminism. Of course, it is right that there are equal opportunities for women, and they need to be campaigned for. But as American feminist Camille Paglia says, *"Stop Blaming Men!"* (You can find her on YouTube.) Men easily become the bad guys in a blanket way that is out of proportion. This is another projection of Saturn, and it doesn't help anyone. It is disempowering for both men and women. It happens with racism too. This is even more dangerous territory to tread. But I was watching a discussion called 'Black Intellectual Roundtable' on YouTube in the wake of the 2020 George Floyd killing in the US. And while not denying there are serious issues to address, these black people were also pointing out the ways in which black people need to look to themselves and not just blame the white people. This is something no white person could say.

It also happens with so-called 'conspiracy theories': people attributing powers to control events that governments, or the supposed secret manipulators behind them, simply do not have. It is not just Saturn that is projected; it can also be described in terms of the other outer planets. The 'spiritual' and protest worlds do not have a shortage of people in denial of their Saturns.

The other one-sidedness of Saturn is the more usual one, and can be seen in an over-emphasis on work and achievement. Of course, achievement is important, in the sense of running with our gifts and making something of them. In a sense, it is what we are here to do. This is Saturn at his best. But then there is the Protestant Work Ethic, where the one-sided Saturn sneaks in with a religious justification behind him. The Protestant Work Ethic, according to Wikipedia

"emphasizes that hard work, discipline, and frugality are a result of a person's subscription to the values espoused by the Protestant faith."

We are still commonly driven by the feeling that hard work is, of itself, virtuous. In other words, we are still driven by some of the values of Christianity even though we may have consciously rejected them. It is interesting that northern Europe and the US tend to be Protestant, and richer, than their southern often more Catholic, neighbours. What a wheeze, turning greed into a religious virtue! This is what Eric Vuillard says about work on the 1st page of his novel *The Order of the Day*:

"... the great, decent fallacy of work, with its small gestures that enfold a silent, conventional truth and reduce the entire epic of our lives to a diligent pantomime."

Work can be an important part of the story of who we are, and in itself that is not a bad thing. The problem is when it is seen as too much of who we are, and the value of doing nothing and dreaming is derided. We feel virtuous just by the facts of being busy and getting up early, and we easily feel guilty if we get up late and just potter around. And yet that pottering around time allows space for the dreaming, for Neptune. But Saturn gets above himself and tries to boss the outer planets around, especially that wet, woolly one, Neptune.

The US has Sun in square to Saturn in its natal chart.

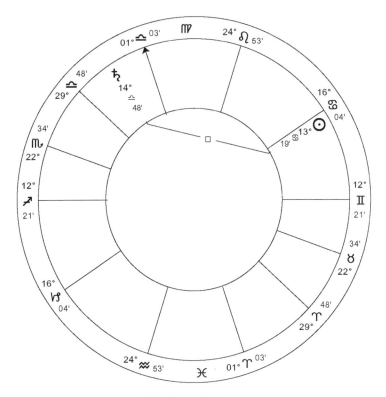

US Sun-Saturn

It is a mixed blessing. That dynamic challenge from Saturn means that you can achieve a tremendous amount. You can build skyscrapers and the world's biggest economy and put a man on the moon. On the other hand, you also build a society where, as the astrologer Liz Greene (who grew up there) puts it, they medicate introverts.

The negative Saturn needs to be turned round from being the denier of the inner life to its guardian: to becoming the walls of the monk's cell, the container for the alchemical transmutation. For the driven worldly achiever, the inner life can easily not exist, and they can sincerely think they are doing dreamy children a favour by medicating them to get them to pay attention in class.

We are brought up to respect and live by the values of the society around us, and that is Saturn, and that is normal and there is nothing, in a sense, wrong with that. Those shared values keep society going. People edit themselves to fit in with this, and for many that is a sacrifice they can tolerate. If, however, there is an individual calling in you that is strong, then you cannot tolerate this sacrifice, and resisting that calling may make you seriously eccentric or even ill. There is an inherent bias in the collective away from those individual values, because they can seem like a threat to orderly existence. And not real. If you're not careful, you can end up as the 'bad guy', as the scapegoat if you cannot accept the 'commonsense' values of society.

For collective humanity, the one-sided Saturn, guardian of society's norms, is adequate. If we find ourselves on a more vocational path – which can happen at any age – then there can be a struggle with Saturn, because that shift does not happen all at once. There is the voice of the collective telling us who we 'should' be (Saturn loves this job) and there is the voice of the Spirit telling is not who we 'should' be but who we are. This conflict can be like a pressure cooker, it can be exactly the 'worthy opponent' needed to push us into a deeper claiming of our own values.

This transition is described well in the film *American Beauty*, in which the main character is a forty-something man who resigns from his executive job, and works instead in a fast-food restaurant while following his fantasies. The film follows the process of him re-finding who he is, and what is of value to him. Meanwhile his wife, who is still a paid-up subscriber to the American Dream, thinks her husband has gone crazy. From a conventional viewpoint, he has indeed gone crazy, in the sense that he no longer subscribes to 'reality' in the form of society's values. But the viewer is led to see that it is really the husband who is the sane one, and the followers of the American Dream – including his homophobic military neighbour – who are the crazy ones. It is messy, but so are these transitions.

In my own chart, Saturn conjoins the Moon and sextiles the

Sun. Saturn is also prominent in the charts of all my immediate family members. The common astrological signatures in a family can be a fascinating study, and the way they may change over the generations. The next generation of my family does not have the same Saturn signature, so I expect there to be less emphasis on worldly achievement.

As an aside, there is a strong fixed emphasis in the charts of both the Queen and Prince Charles, the current and future monarchs of the UK, which is what you would expect in people who are the upholders of a long tradition. Prince William, however, who will succeed Prince Charles as monarch, does not have this emphasis, so we may expect to see some kind of major change associated with his accession to the throne. The astrologer Bernadette Brady has pointed out that an eclipse series that began at the start of the English monarchy will be coming to an end in the coming decades. So, these two factors together could be pointing towards the end of the monarchy as we know it.

I have spent years on the Saturnian anvil: valuing, on the one hand, the ability he gives me to get things done and to become competent at what I do; and on the other hand, distancing myself from Saturn as the guy with the big stick, standing over my shoulder, telling me I am only what I do and sometimes, in an unguarded moment, sneaking in and telling me I have failed dreadfully at my life in terms of what I was 'meant' to be doing, i.e., running a successful business. These different voices in myself, which I think we all have one way or the other, and are like the grit in the oyster. They send us on a voyage of self-discovery and self-unfoldment, if only because life would be too painful to do otherwise.

Moon-Saturn aspects can describe adult responsibility (Saturn) in childhood (Moon.) The Dalai Lama has Moon opposite Saturn. From a very early age he was recognised as an incarnate Lama, and went to live with the monks (as Neptune opposed his

MC). He still saw his mother, but adult responsibilities loomed large. However, he seems to have come out of it fine.

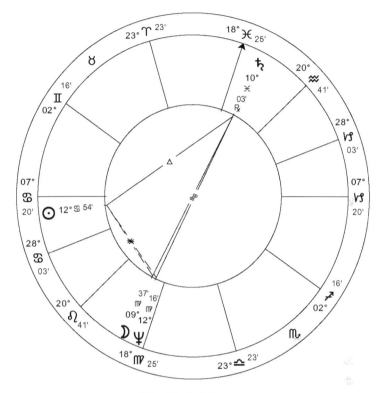

The Dalai Lama

This is why I am using the Dalai Lama as an example, because we can sometimes assume there has to be a lasting problem with this aspect. All the astrology does is show us what happened. It does not tell us how the individual responded to it.

My own Moon-Saturn describes being sent to boarding school aged eight, as transiting Pluto was squaring my Moon. The boarding school system in England is set up to give children a head-start in the world, and of course if you are eight, that is too young. You are still in the childhood Moon phase. If Pluto is squaring the Moon when this occurs, the outcome is unlikely to be a good one. There is a disruption in the relationship with the mother (Moon). The Moon is also our emotional life and development, so that too is easily disrupted. But not always, as the case of the Dalai Lama seems to show.

You never know how challenging aspects are going to play out in the life of an individual. In medieval times, planets and aspects were divided into good and bad. I am not going to rush in and judge that from a modern perspective. But we do have an element of choice about how we live our lives that they did not have. We can find ways of living that suit our astrology. Mars in Pisces can be a submarine commander!

However, the hard aspects also describe inner challenges, and if the individual does not want to address them, then they may well see them as 'bad'. As Jung put it, that which we do not want to become conscious of appears from without as Fate. One man I knew had a Moon-Neptune conjunction. Capable as a businessman, he had no interest in what was happening within himself. He remained naïve about women to the end of his days, having effectively bought himself a second, and much younger, wife. Everyone could see she was using him. This is the Moon (wife) and Neptune (delusion). In a more consciously inclined man, a Moon-Neptune conjunction would give the potential for heightened sensitivity and intuition, a fineness of feeling and connection to otherworldly realms. But he was quite happy to remain unconscious in this respect.

So back to Saturn. Someone else with a Moon-Saturn opposition like the Dalai Lama's could have spent their life separated from their own feeling nature, and feeling oppressed by the expectations that their parents or society had for them. Either way, Moon-Saturn always has the potential for mastery of the emotional realm. I don't mean mastery in the sense of dominating the emotions – although one is likely to do that to start with, dividing them up into what one 'ought' and 'ought not' to be feeling. What I mean by mastery is the hard-won ability to live with our emotions, to tolerate who we are, which then leaves room for the gradual process of transformation to occur.

Saturn shows this potential for mastery in whatever area he appears. If we are outwardly inclined, then this can be quite straightforward, although it can be at the expense of inner values. America is a good case in point. Her Sun square Saturn shows the country's mastery of the world. But the Sun is in the sign of Cancer, and their struggles with healthcare, of properly taking care of their people, are well known. If America were to build the best healthcare system in the world, then it would have fulfilled its Sun square Saturn. An individual attempting to be conscious might achieve this. But it is very difficult for collectives to become conscious, and their charts are much more likely as a result to play out as Fate (see Chapter 16 Are We Fated?)

Saturn doesn't show just a potential for mastery, he shows a requirement to do so if we are to feel fulfilled. It usually takes a long time with Saturn. His is the wisdom and experience that have been earned over time. Sometimes it can show precocity, an old head on young shoulders. Einstein had a Mercury-Saturn conjunction in Aries, and he was able to come out with profound, ground-breaking ideas at a young age. And then he seemed to get stuck there, unable to accept the ideas of quantum physics. This is Saturn as Senex, the archetype of the old man who cannot let in new life.

Saturn is pivotal. He is the planet that pushes and shoves us, often reluctantly, to incarnate, to bring spirit into matter. This is the message of the central symbol of Christian culture, the Crucifix: Christ (Spirit) impaled on the Cross (Matter). It is painful. Even if we are not Christian – and perhaps most of us aren't – we are deluding ourselves if we do not understand that the Christian mythology still profoundly influences our conceptions of life. Hence the Protestant Work Ethic, a compulsion that many of us suffer from, and its largely unconscious religious roots. In the same way, the idea that life is a process of spirit incarnating into matter, and the resistance that the spirit feels to doing that, carries a lot of power for us.

When we bring Spirit into Matter, we are incarnating Uranus, Neptune and Pluto. They are the Spirit under three different aspects: creativity, imagination and power respectively. Neptune is perhaps Spirit in its most typically understood sense, and Saturn finds it very tempting to try to boss Neptune around. Saturn wants to take charge of this divine impulse, to create rules for it, and to tell you which days are holy and what God does and doesn't want you to eat and who you are allowed to have sex with and so on. It is Saturn doing this, but as ever it is also us doing this, because we want to be told what to do and what to believe. That is natural for partially-formed humanity, and it is a need that life – and the outer planet transits – will wean us off, over time, if we are willing.

The outer planets cannot be bossed around by Saturn, because they are outside his orbit. Sure, his job is to ensure the planets within his orbit incarnate, that they get their acts together. But his job is to be receptive to, to be the servant of, a bridge for, the energies of the outer planets.

Saturn is a kingly archetype, he is proud, and the humility to be the servant doesn't always come easily to him. He can, in a way, succeed in bossing around the outer planets, but the results are not pretty. With Uranus, he produces rebels without a cause and mindless anti-authoritarianism; a squashed Neptune, desperate for an experience of spirit, easily turns to alcohol and drugs; and Pluto may become an abuser, or the victim of abuse.

Whatever it is that torments us may have its roots in a hard aspect between Saturn and an outer planet, or indeed between any of the inner planets and an outer planet. All aspects of our conscious personality have this need to become receptive to something bigger than themselves, that is really calling the shots. Our job as astrologers is to discern and help navigate this process in the people who come to us. There are riches to be found once we can let go of the survival self, which is necessarily quite narrow and rigid and trying to stay in control, and begin to let ourselves be guided from elsewhere. This is a process of listening and of trust, and of courage too, which is lifelong. There is no limit to it, because the outer planets do not have limits.

The second Saturn Return comes at around the age of 58. Schematically, we have spent the 30 years since the first Saturn Return incarnating, fully arriving in the world through all the responsibilities we have been taking. And then the second Saturn Return comes along, and we can begin to let go of all that. There is nothing to prove any more. As the playwright John Mortimer put it, we don't have to pretend to be an adult anymore.

I think this is the point at which we can seriously begin to turn Saturn around from being the boss of the inner planets to being the servant of the outer planets. It is the beginning of becoming an Elder. We have the hard-earned, earthly wisdom of 30 years of incarnating Saturn, as well as the unearned, otherworldly wisdom of the outer planets on our doorstep.

Saturn is intimately associated with the Protestant Work Ethic (and the Chinese have their Confucian Work Ethic, the key difference being that for the Chinese, it is collective rather than individual achievement that matters most.) I have seen people after they retire – some years after the 2nd Saturn Return – unable to stop. The work ethic – "you must keep busy" – is a like a wheel that keeps spinning, and then gradually begins to slow down. I think it is good to make a point sometimes of just pottering, or doing nothing, and getting up late, and living with the discomfort, the guilt, the inadequacy, that often produces. There is a different way of valuing who we are to be found in that discomfort, that is liberating and replete with meaning.

The period after the 2nd Saturn Return can, paradoxically, be the time of the greatest, the most meaningful achievements. The period between the 1st and 2nd Saturn Returns has made us an adequate vehicle for the Spirit, and with nothing to 'prove' any more (in an ideal world) there is space for the outer planets to have their say. It can almost be like what we were really born to do. Saturn feels sufficiently secure to turn his gaze outwards, and receive the creative energies of Uranus, the imaginative energies of Neptune, and the transformative, life giving energies of Pluto. The signs of the zodiac are ruled by different planets, and those planets give us information as to the nature of those signs. Saturn rules both Capricorn and Aquarius (in traditional astrology, before the outer planets came along.) Saturn ruling Capricorn is straightforward enough. Capricorns are typically ambitious and capable, and rise high in their professions. They are also typically quite conservative, because the rules work for them and for society, producing the order, security and stability that Capricorns value. They also value responsibility, and have the hard-earned wisdom to become leaders in the community.

But what about Aquarius, that other sign rules by Saturn? I think the clue lies in the fact that they are adjacent signs. Capricorn, in other words, grows into Aquarius, just as any sign grows into the next one along, and grows out of the one behind. I think this is an under-studied phenomenon: the adjacency of two signs can mean we overlook their connection, because there is no major aspect, such as a square or a sextile, between them.

Aquarius is in many ways the opposite of Capricorn: one values conformity, the other rebellion. But it is only an apparent opposition. Through his mastery of the rules, Capricorn earns the right to break them, and so becomes Aquarius. Both signs have the Saturnian sense of responsibility to the community. But the emphasis for Capricorn is the past, upholding that which has been established; for Aquarius the emphasis is the future, how do things need to change? Right and left wing politics, if you like.

This shift in emphasis is akin to the second Saturn Return. If you like, Saturn becomes more Aquarian after the second return, building on what has come before, but more open to new ideas, and willing to let go of that which is no longer useful.

The shadow side of Saturn as ruler of Capricorn is the Senex, the old man who wants to keep everything as it has always been, and will not let in new life. The shadow side of Saturn as ruler of Aquarius is the *Puer*, the Peter Pan, who is secretly afraid of authority and protests against it for that reason. If you like, it is the shadow of right and left wing politics respectively. Each wing has something to offer, yet each wing tends to undervalue and to demonise the other.

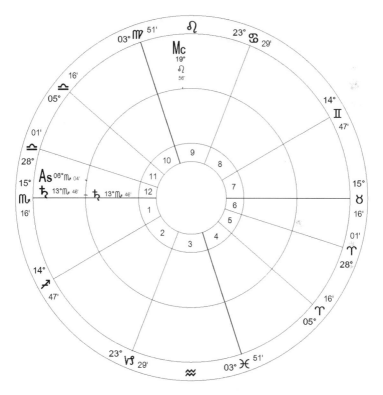

Margaret Thatcher

As Margaret Thatcher, the UK Prime Minister from 1979 to 1990, came up to her second Saturn Return in 1983, she won a landslide General Election victory, and soon set about taking on, and defeating, the miners. This was a turning point in the power that the unions had over government in the UK, which had brought down the previous Conservative administration. Thatcher came into her own at this period.

It is not my job as an astrologer to stand in judgement over Thatcher's actions. She is the most divisive UK Prime Minister of modern times. But what I will say is that astrology teaches us to stand back and observe these events, without judgement, otherwise we cannot do the astrology. I discussed this earlier in the Chapter 3 on Bad Astrology, and I think it is worth repeating, because it is something so many of us find so hard. People often don't seem to realise that they are being judgemental, and that it is not possible to do astrology, when they talk about, for example, Thatcher or Trump as awful people, as though those are facts. They are judgements, understandable ones probably, but they are not facts. And it is clear from the facts and from the astrology that Thatcher was coming into her own, she was firmly on her throne. Not only that, but she had the power of the collective running through her. She had won the Falklands War and a general election, and was about to oversee the clash of two great collective forces in the country. Which means that outer planet influence, which Saturn becomes more open to at this time, was also present.

I think it is instructive to look back to Thatcher's 1st Saturn Return in 1954-55. This was the time when she was struggling to become an MP. She had had a series of defeats, either in elections, or in being chosen as candidate, and in 1955 chose not to stand in that year's general election, partly because her twins were two years old, and she felt she needed to prioritise them. This is all classic 1st Saturn Return stuff. The responsibilities of motherhood, and the struggle to establish a career. It is a very different flavour to the second Saturn Return 29 years later, where her career is well-established, and she reaches the pinnacle of her power and success.

Chapter 14

Uranus, Neptune and Pluto

The nature of these planets has unfolded to a great extent throughout the course of this book. This section will be used to complete whatever hasn't been said so far.

At the beginning of Chapter 12, on Creation Mythologies, I spoke about the roles of Uranus, Neptune and Pluto in the Big Bang. Uranus had the idea for a universe and lit the blue touch paper, Pluto provided the power to make it happen, and Neptune was the primordial imagination that dreamed the forms of the universe into being. But it's not like they did their Big Bang and then walked off to do something else. Those three forces remain very active, indeed fundamental, in the universe at large, as well as in the lives of individual people.

The function of Uranus is to shake us out of the habitual ways of being that are basic to human nature: those ways serve a purpose, but they also hinder new growth. If you have a prominent Uranus, you will never feel entirely at ease living within conventional values. You will easily feel trapped, and doing or thinking things that subvert those values, even without meaning to. You are the trickster. There is a coldness to Uranus: he doesn't mind separating you from all that feels warm and connected and comfortable in order to expose you to some wider truths. And he cannot be controlled: if you try too hard to fit in and continue in a 'responsible' way you will find yourself doing or saying exactly the wrong thing, and wondering how that happened. Like all the outer planets, we have to learn to trust them and bow to them. Then on a fundamental level it will feel like our life is working, that it is where it is meant to be, even though there will probably also be the usual level of things that aren't working very well.

Uranus is the Red Pill from *The Matrix* (see Chapter 3). I experienced Uranus as the Red Pill in 1998. He was opposite my natal Uranus and conjunct my Mercury, my mind. And the closed Buddhist system I had been in for 18 years started to shatter. I think most of us live in closed systems to one degree or another, so there is no shame in owning it, if you can see it, which most of us can't. The closed system we live in seems like reality itself, which is why anyone who disagrees can appear to us like they have something wrong with them. The ideas we hold about reality aren't necessarily 'wrong': the Buddhist ideas I held at the time had a lot going for them, many of them were profound, and they had helped me unfold something in myself. Fortunately, some of the ideas were a bit squiffy – the Buddhist teacher had his biases, like most of us do – and they were my way out. The areas in which I had disagreed for some time started to really matter to me. It was like lightning, lighting up the landscape in a very different way, and then retreating.

Uranus is not an emotional planet, he tends to function more cognitively (as reflected in his co-rulership of Aquarius) and we can need to do catch-up with our emotions afterwards, as I had to. It took me several years to catch up properly with what Uranus had shown me, even though I acted on his insights quite quickly. What Uranus was doing fundamentally was awakening me to my own autonomous powers of judgement, my own inner guidance. For that to happen, we need to separate ourselves from the collective understandings and values with which we tend to surround ourselves. Uranus has a necessary surgical quality in this respect.

As I said earlier, everyone thinks they are autonomous, that their thoughts are their own, and if you own up to your own shortcomings in this area, you are likely to attract condescension! But look how vulnerable we are to criticism, and to what others think of us. We are nearly all extremely fragile in this respect. The 'alternative' community, the 'counter-culture' can be just as conformist as conventional society: many people here get their identity from a rigid opposition to, and mistrust of that which is conventional. It can be a step along the way, but eventually we need to make our peace with conventional society: that does not mean subscribing to all its values, but not judging it too harshly, because it is made up of regular humans doing what regular humans have always done. This rigid oppositional stance is part of the shadow-side of Uranus. I think it often points to something unresolved in our own background, that is being kept at bay. It is usually an unconscious process.

The Uranus journey towards autonomy is lifelong. There is deep guidance to be found within ourselves, but it takes time, we need to be ready for it. Even then, when it erupts it can be quite destructive at times, and can take a while to catch up.

The separation and isolation that Uranus seems to create is more apparent than real. On a surface level, he does indeed separate us from received opinions and values, and the feeling of belonging and acceptance that comes with participating in them – which is just the usual human lot. But that sense of belonging and acceptance is illusory from the point of view of our souls, because there is little room for who we really are.

This is where we start to move into Neptune's territory. Neptune connects us to the whole of existence. On a literal, physical level, we may be on our own due to the actions of Uranus. But then Neptune reveals that infinite matrix that is our real belonging. To the extent that we cling on for security to the tribe, to that extent it is difficult to experience the existential interconnectedness and love for all of life that Neptune offers.

Neptune is associated with anything that alters or heightens consciousness, including drugs. Research into the effects of psychedelics has started in recent years, after a gap of decades. The research was originally stopped for the same reason that dancing was proscribed in churches in the Middle Ages. It gives people their own connection to the divine, which means they move away from the norms and the control of society, and that is experienced as a threat. LSD was demonised.

The recent research that I have encountered uses psilocybin, the active ingredient in magic mushrooms, at John Hopkins University in the USA. They are getting some remarkable results, but what I find most remarkable is the fact that the research is happening at all, and in such an august and conservative setting. It speaks volumes for the talents of the lead researcher, Roland Griffiths. There is a great discussion on the subject between him and Jordan Peterson on YouTube. It seems that Harvard University, another august and conservative institution, has a programme for creating a psychedelic chaplaincy.

One of the weaknesses of the objective, scientific approach for this kind of experiment is that with psychedelics, surroundings and context matter, and the lab setting is not necessarily the most conducive. I think one of the strengths of the academic approach is the articulation and categorisation of the experiences, such that they are able to discern the most important common threads. Volunteers typically experience interconnectedness, like we're all in this together; a sense of the preciousness of the experience; and a level of meaning. All of which can mean they end up rewriting the narrative they have about themselves and their place in the world. Many of the volunteers describe it as the single most important experience of their lives.

When I heard this description, I thought well that is a good description of the function of Neptune, with or without psychedelics. Having been separated from, or even torn from, our immersion in the collective consciousness of the group by Uranus, we become ready for the Neptune initiation. Neptune awakens us from the dream of literal, collective existence into how things really are.

Uranus, Aquarius and the 11th house are associated with community, particularly of the alternative or idealistic variety. However, I don't think they can easily create community in its full sense: a bunch of rebels, maybe, who define themselves as much by what they are against as what they are for. But it is not a stable situation, that can put down deep roots. It does, however, get the ball rolling. The interconnectedness of Neptune, rather than the separation of Uranus, is needed to create something lasting, and here we are moving into the 12th House, which is community in its widest sense.

I think it is important not to idealise community, and bemoan its lack. Community in the ordinary sense is necessary for the survival of collective humanity. It provides belonging, relationship, security, recognition, values to live by....... but it can be suffocating if you have a calling within you, some other source of meaning and authority that you need to live by.

Imagine being in a small country community a few hundred years ago, with limited opportunities as to what you could do with your life, and the local priest keeping an eye on your morals. That may well have been fine for most people, but for the few with some other calling, and nowhere to go, it could have driven them crazy, unless they had what it took to just leave and make a life for themselves in a freer environment.

I doubt there has ever been much in the way of community for people with an individual calling. Nowadays we have it really good: we may well have a few friends, maybe in far-flung places, who we can talk to from the point of view of what gives our lives meaning. I suspect that it probably as good as it has ever been.

Neptune can be the mob consciousness of which we have become very wary in modern times – the Nazis are the obvious example. There are also football crowds. The reason it is Neptune is because in these situations there is a loss of individual consciousness and submersion in the blind will of a collective. A collective that is threatened or insecure in some way is prepared to believe anything that a leader tells them. No evidence is required.

In the 2020 US election, millions of people were prepared

to believe that the American election had been stolen, yet there was never any evidence to substantiate that. Even five months after the election, three-quarters of Republicans believed this. That is really worth paying attention to: it says to me that most people are prepared to believe whatever suits them. Facts do not count for anything when there is a strong need to believe. This is the shadow of Neptune: the loss of self, but in this case into something less than, rather than more than, human.

Collective consciousness has a bad rap in modern times, even though most of us are immersed in it without knowing. But there is another kind of collective consciousness, and there is a word for it that comes from the Russian Orthodox Church: Sobornost. It is community at its best, and you find it in Ceremony. It is the kind of collective consciousness that occurs when those present have shared individual values, and in which the sense of collectivity heightens, rather than diminishes, the sense of individuality. There is a synergy between self and other.

A sweatlodge (a kind of ceremonial sauna) might be a good example. You may not personally know the people you are sweating with. But in a sweatlodge, we are brought back to essentials, all the 'add-ons' by which we usually identify ourselves are gone: we are in the dark, wearing nothing or very little, close to the elements, and focussing our minds on that which is of most value to us. There can be a sense of deep connection on a Spirit level with the other people in the lodge, which heightens that sense of connection to Spirit that we are, on an individual level, focussed on. That is Sobornost. It is a beautiful thing. It may occur in a 'sharing circle', where people are attempting to be true to their experience, and not fearing that others present will judge them. Or in a prayer ceremony, where people take turns in having a conversation with the natural world, and talk in a heartfelt way about their lives.

Sobornost can happen on a one-to-one level also, where two people are being authentic, maybe even having quite a 'difficult' conversation as a result, but that honesty comes from a shared sense of being true to the Spirit.

Even then, people usually only want honesty up to a point. They are sticking their heads out of the collective mindset, but it is tentative, and we are liable to recreate collective mindsets around our 'spiritual' communities. It is inevitable to a degree, and it has to be danced around. It is where the trickster has her role: pushing these kinds of collectives by breaking the rules, by speaking for the elephant under the carpet that everybody is pretending is not there. And you will not be thanked by some people. I once got blocked from two of the biggest Facebook shamanic groups for saying we shouldn't put indigenous people on pedestals: but not before a considerable number of people had expressed their appreciation to me for saying it. For others, it was like I had insulted the Pope.

So Uranus helps us break away from immersion in collective consciousness, as something that is truly our own begins to emerge; Neptune can then replace the old, limited sense of belonging to a group with a sense of belonging to the whole of life. This is an ecstatic and meaningful experience, that can change the whole narrative of our life, as the psychedelic research has shown. Neptune can bring us into the solitude of his 12th House, in which we realise that, far from being on our own, we contain the whole universe.

If you have a pronounced Neptune, Pisces or 12th house in your chart, there will always be a pull towards this universal type of experience, in which the ordinary self dissolves. You will only know who you are by not trying to create an identity, in its ordinary sense, for yourself. There is a push from society to create such an identity, and poor old Pisces/Neptune/12th house people can feel like failures for not measuring up. They may spend half their lives trying to work out what they will do when they 'grow up'. But it can be exactly this sort of pressure over a long period, painful as it is, that pushes us to own who we are.

Going back to the Big Bang analogy, Uranus lit the blue touch paper that began this completely new idea called a universe. In the same way, Uranus catalyses a new paradigm in our lives that we could never have thought of: that is why he is creative, what he does is never merely a re-arrangement of the old, but the introduction of some new element of consciousness around which the rest of our being needs, in time, to be re-ordered.

Neptune is the primordial imagination which dreams into being the forms and symmetries and beauties of a universe. In the same way, Neptune reveals that new paradigm, which Uranus has catalysed, to be one of connection to the whole universe, with ourselves at its centre. We each contain the universe. Time and space are illusions in Neptune's world.

Neptune is also the winds of Spirit that blow through us, showing us how to live, what to do, what passions to follow. He is arguably the presiding deity of divinatory astrology, the idea that astrology is essentially an intuitive art, that its insights come from outside the usual mind and five senses through which we operate, but which can be used to substantiate those otherworldly insights.

Not all astrologers would agree with this. There are those who prioritise what the tradition tells us are the meanings within the chart. Of course, those are true as well, but it is a matter of emphasis, and this is something you can feel in the way an astrologer approaches the subject. Whatever they might say, you can feel whether their main source of authority is exoteric – the tradition as passed down, available to all – or esoteric, inner, what the spirit is whispering to them in its passionate way. It is the difference between religion and spirituality, and there is no neat dividing line: often our lives are a slow process of moving from the former to the latter. It is a dialectic one finds in all religions between the orthodox, exoteric mainstream and the mystical – sometimes heretical – minorities. Heresy comes from the Greek *haireomai* meaning to choose: it means you are free, that you cannot be controlled.

I realised as I was writing this book that I have written it in a divinatory way. I swung in and out of self-doubt during the weeks of writing. After all, shouldn't a book have a clear theme around which all the material is clearly organised, and shouldn't there be references from the tradition that substantiate any claims I have made about astrology? Well, yes. And no! A book can be written in a rational, clearly organised way, and there is obvious value in that. But like anything, there can be both 'classical' and 'romantic' ways. The classical ways, steeped in tradition, will tend to be in the majority. The romantic ways give primacy to intuition and feeling as the guiding principle. A novelist writing in a classical way will plan much of his book out beforehand: what the plot is, who the characters are etc. A novelist writing in a romantic way will just start writing, and see where it leads, guided by an initial compulsion to put pen to paper. She will probably be continually surprised by where the plot goes and the characters that appear. Any novelist is probably a mixture of these two modus operandi, and there is no right or wrong between them.

So, I wrote this book in that divinatory way, which is to give primacy to the promptings of the spirit. I would finish one theme, and out of that would tumble another that I wanted to write about, and then sometimes out would tumble a theme I had already written about, but wanting me to say more. And so it has gone on. Neptune has presided over this creation. It has been like being in freefall, and learning to trust that.

When you work in an intuitive or divinatory way, there is always an element of risk involved. You do not have the tradition to fall back on, to wave at your readers to say look what I am saying is true, because some venerable other also said it! Hence the self-doubt. There is only one thing worse than having self-doubt, and that is not having any. Self-doubt is a mixed thing: partly it can be childhood stuff, and we just need to hold its hand.

But it is also an edge, a cliff-top on which we are balanced without support, relying on the truthfulness, the reality of what we are saying, to be its support. This is the divinatory path: it is like removing the stabilisers from the bike when you were a kid, and finding you are fine, that you in fact have more freedom of movement than before, and that you are a better cyclist. And we do this again and again: we keep taking steps outside the authority of tradition, we doubt ourselves, but it works, and we come to trust incrementally more that power that is within us. Writing this book has been very much that sort of process, but I did not realise that was what I was doing until near the end. Sometimes we just push on with something we feel we have to do, with the shadow of self-doubt in the background, and then moments come when we experience the reward of giving birth to ourselves in a new way, a more confident way, without necessarily realising that that was what we were doing all along. Transformation often has this character, that we can only see its nature when we look back, that the challenging time that seemed to be going on and on was building something below the surface that eventually revealed itself.

Between them, Uranus, Neptune and Pluto describe three different ways in which Spirit, the deeper reality behind conventional, convenient truths reveals itself, or even forces its way in. Pluto is the raw power of life, that will not be resisted, pushing on to its next unfoldment.

This is where the evolutionary astrologers are on to something, for they see Pluto as the main driver of our evolutionary unfoldment. He certainly represents the power and necessity of it. Their mistake is in assuming an overall, progressive design which can be discerned in the chart, that is called 'evolution'. We can find anything we want in the chart if we look hard enough. What I think demands the most rigour is in being honest about what we do and do not know on our pulses, and staying close to that. The mystery can then reveal itself in ways that it can't if we bring our merely human ideas to the table.

What Pluto shows us is that life is always moving on and renewing. Sure, I can perceive a qualitative difference to that unfoldment during the course of my life. That is a bit of linearity within the greater context of the cycle of birth and death. Linearity is a useful discerning tool, belonging to the air element, but it is a servant of the whole, which is a circle, it is cyclical, and includes all four elements. To extrapolate that linearity beyond this lifetime is pure conjecture, it is not something we experience. I think we can be pretty confident that the self as we know it largely dissolves at death – else why would we be afraid? – which makes absurd the idea of positing an unfoldment of that temporary self over lifetimes.

All we know is that Pluto is continually moving us on to a fresh unfoldment, much as he moves life on to produce new species: it is our human judgement that one species is more 'advanced' than another.

For me, Pluto is a 'shamanic' planet, inasmuch as he demands we pay attention to the earth, to our bodies, to our viscera, and understand that our true power comes from listening in that kind of way. Reality is here, not up in the sky, as Christianity taught us. And Capricorn is a shamanic sign, in that it is both earth and cardinal: cardinal begins, initiates, transforms, while the earth element emphasis the context of the natural world, which is the starting point for shamanism. Earth Magic. Pluto is arguably exalted in Capricorn for this reason.

Going back to the Big Bang analogy – or mythology – Pluto provides the power for the universe to happen. In the same way, a Pluto transit often involves claiming our power, claiming something within ourselves whose time has come to be lived, and may well have been causing us misery until we claimed it. We find the courage to live from a fuller sense of who we are. That new person may not be the person that everyone around us wants – or needs us – to be. You can find this in relationships, where each partner has the power in certain ways: it is an unconscious contract. And then one person starts to wake up, they start to need to become more whole, and live the power that the other was carrying. Maybe the man has given over his emotional authority to the woman, or maybe the man is the one who earns and controls the money. However it pans out – it is often stereotypical, but by no means always – the other person's settled universe is being severely disrupted; it can seem like reality itself is being assaulted. So, this is why Pluto's power can need claiming, because it may well be opposed by others. But often, with hindsight, that opposition was exactly what was needed to provide the pressure to claim that new self.

Neptune and Pluto, being the two outermost planets, are the two big transformers. Astrologers are guided in their interpretations of Pluto transits by the story of Pluto's abduction of Prosperpina, which was described in Chapter 5. The first part of a Pluto transit can indeed feel like an abduction, in which a large part of your energy has gone elsewhere. Leaving you with enough to keep life going, but no more. Meanwhile, deep below ground, a slow and secret alchemy is taking place, old structures of the psyche are being taken apart to provide room, and to provide compost, for the new life that will eventually push through the surface. It is winter-time, and one of the main jobs of an astrologer at these times can be to reassure the client that all is OK beneath the surface, the wasteland they may be experiencing is not something to be struggled against, but to be trusted. It may mean you end up doing less for a while, and questions as to your value in your own and other's eyes may be raised if you cannot be active in the old way.

Pluto – and Neptune, for he can have a similar effect – push us to go deeper in our valuing of ourselves. This is what the bleak period of a transit can teach us. Nor is it about waiting for the transit to be over so that you can then carry on in the same old way – which is often what clients mean when they ask when the transit will be over. Society is inevitably biased towards outer performance when it judges us, while Pluto and Neptune ask us to ignore that – which is a very big ask – and to value ourselves according to whether we are being true to that calling within. Being true to that calling may mean doing very little for long periods, and tuning into and trusting that deeper alchemy that is beyond our control.

We have a commonly understood myth for Pluto transits, but not so for Neptune. Maybe that is appropriate, that we have nothing we can grasp hold of, we are left floundering.

I think, though, that a Neptune transit can be just as much of an Underworld as a Pluto transit. In both transits, ordinary life with its goals and drives is to some extent suspended and you are taken somewhere else for transformation, an inner place, and this can go on for years, it becomes your way of life. In the case of Pluto, it is an earthy Underworld where your building blocks are demolished and replaced. With Neptune, it is a watery Underworld where you are gradually washed away and absorbed into the greater consciousness around you.

It is interesting that the two crucibles of transformation should be earth and water, the still, steady containing elements.

With Pluto you are abducted, with Neptune you are shipwrecked and drowned. (Or maddened. Or possessed). And then after a while this happens:

"Full fathom five thy father lies;
Of his bones are coral made;
Those are pearls that were his eyes;
Nothing of him that does fade,
But doth suffer a sea-change
Into something rich and strange."

These lines are from Shakespeare's *The Tempest*, and I think they are a good metaphor for a Neptune transit. With both Pluto and

Neptune, we are taken apart and rebuilt, but I think they have different flavours. I have spent some time trying to work them out psychoanalytically, Pluto does this to you and Neptune does that, but I'm not sure how possible that is.

What happens to us under these transits is essentially a story that has a feel to it. We went somewhere else and we came back different. The fairies took us away. Something out there took our soul away, and our soul is us, and we went to this other place with these people and we can never be the same again because we have seen this other place. It may be the Dark Earth we have tasted. Or we encountered an Angel:

> *"Who, if I cried out, who among the angelic hierarchies*
> *would hear me? and even if one of them pressed me*
> *suddenly against his heart: I would be consumed*
> *in that overwhelming existence"*
> (Rilke: 1st *Duino Elegy*)

Paradoxically, we only belong here on the planet, we only incarnate, after we have been taken by Pluto or Neptune, abducted or shipwrecked, and then killed, dead to life as we knew it, and then reborn with that look in our eyes, telling of that strange faraway place that is always with us. Goethe:

> *"And so long as you haven't experienced*
> *this: to die and so to grow,*
> *you are only a troubled guest*
> *on the dark earth."*

My real learning of astrology was under the series of Pluto transits I had for about ten years from the early 90s onwards. As an adult, I did not have major Neptune transits until the mid-noughties onwards, so I always had to confess that I did not know, for myself, what these transits were about, though of course I could always extrapolate from what I had read, but that isn't the same thing. They began with Neptune conjoining my Sun in 2008/9. Much had been activated in the year or two leading up to that, as I began my astrology blog and wrote my way in to my own, original understanding of astrology. I began to surf the galactic highways!

There was an element of floundering beginning in my life as a whole, but that didn't seriously begin until 2012, when Neptune started the long process of hard-aspecting my Angles, Moon and Saturn. At the time of writing (2021) that process is not complete, as Neptune will square my Saturn in 2022. Below is what I wrote in 2015, while I was on the one hand being swamped by Neptune, but on the other experiencing a new level of soulfulness, of calling, within myself. This is how these transits often go: we experience new gifts coming in at the same time as being taken apart.

"Under my Pluto transits, I was always planning the next thing, doing it for a bit, then being taken apart. By the time it came to the Neptune transits, I was willing to flounder and not know where I was going in a way that I wouldn't have been able to were it not for Pluto. That doesn't mean it's been easy. But there has nevertheless been a flow as long as I'm not fighting what's happening. My blog has flowed over the last seven years, it has shaped me in a way nothing else ever has (it seems). And I have done it in a Neptunian way, I have written as and when I feel like it.

"Of his bones are coral made;
Those are pearls that were his eyes…"

Neptune has dissolved me, and in has come coral and pearl from the surrounding oceanic consciousness. An ocean of riches, if you allow Neptune to shipwreck you. And while Pluto kept defeating the guy in the back room, Neptune has dissolved the wall between us so I can now start to see him.

There is also the madness of Neptune transits. With Pluto we are abducted by a god, with Neptune we are possessed by a god (when we're not being shipwrecked!) With Pluto, elements of the psyche that need to come on board present themselves as demons. Our job is not to slay them but to learn to live with them. With Neptune, these elements can take us over, we see reality through the eyes of the unlived soul part, and to others' eyes it can seem like we've gone mad, which in a way we have. And the job is to live the main personality and the new bit together, rather than switching between the two. And Neptune, the dissolver of barriers, will do that for you.

That is one of the great things about these two planets: there are some big jobs to do, but they will do them for you. We couldn't possibly know what to do anyway. Our part is to be patient and to stay with whatever's happening, maybe over years. If big parts of your life don't work anymore, or if you have no idea where you're headed, that is probably fine, that is probably as it needs to be, and you just need to stay with it for however many years it lasts.

In 2007, as I was beginning my long encounter with Neptune, I wrote a piece called A Myth for Neptune Transits. And it was the madness aspect of the transits that I focussed on. Below is what I wrote:

I Googled 'god of illusion' and the 1st result I got was Dionysus, who Liz Greene promotes as a strongly Piscean figure in her book *The Astrology of Fate*. In particular (p263), there is the story of Dionysus and King Pentheus.

As a young man Dionysus had been driven mad by Zeus' jealous wife Hera.

"He went wandering all over the world, accompanied by his tutor... and a company of wild Maenads. He taught the art of the vine to Egypt and India, and then returned to wander around Greece.

Eventually he arrived at Thebes, the place of his mother's birth. There King Pentheus... disliked the god's dissolute appearance, and arrested him and his shabby train. But Dionysus drove the king mad, and Pentheus found that he had shackled a bull instead of the god. The Maenads escaped and went raging out upon the mountains, where they tore wild animals in pieces. The King attempted to stop them but, inflamed with wine and religious ecstasy, the Maenads, led by the King's mother, rent him limb from limb and tore off his head. Thus he met the same fate as the god whom he had rejected."

And from Wikipedia:

"The female worshippers of Dionysus were known as Maenads, who often experienced divine ecstasy. Pentheus was slowly driven mad by the compelling Dionysus, and lured to the woods of Mount Cithaeron to see the Maenads. When the women spied Pentheus, they tore him to pieces like they did earlier in the play to a herd of cattle. Brutally, his head was torn off by his mother Agave as he begged for his life."

We could say that the essence of a Neptune transit is possession by the god. This is different to a Pluto transit, where you could say the essence is abduction by the god, and being brought to his underworld. Apparently, this was one of the unusual characteristics of the worship of Dionysus in Roman times, that he was experienced internally i.e., you were possessed.

The Maenads themselves are a graphic description of what happens when you surrender to the god: there is an experience of ecstasy as the normal inhibitions and controlling, rational will are no longer present. OK, they also tear animals and even people to pieces, but this is symbolic of the ecstatic freedom of primal consciousness, and the radical dissolution of ordinary, ego consciousness under a Neptune transit: you are torn to pieces, in particular your head is torn off by your mother! You are no longer in control (head), and this allows an experience of a primal, source consciousness (mother), that actually takes care of us (mother), and the transit is about learning to let more of that in to our daily lives. And it's not like we have a choice. What happened to Pentheus is also a description of what happens when you resist Neptune/Dionysus, when you refuse, like Pentheus, to worship him. You get torn apart by mad women!

So, the essence of a Neptune transit is surrender to this god, becoming a 'walk-in' if you like! If you oppose him, you'll be torn apart – and this will be the difficult part of the transit, because we all have our sides that want to remain in control. But this is also deeply transformative. And to the extent that we surrender, there is an initiation into his ecstatic realm. There was a long tradition of mystery cults around Dionysus, but very little is known about them. This is appropriate, for his realm is esoteric and beyond words, and people who have been there speak about it guardedly, if at all. Another reason for the secrecy is that this sort of experience/ behaviour is felt as deeply threatening by conventional society. Hence the opposition that Dionysus regularly encountered. Hence, perhaps, the official opposition to 'rave' culture in the UK. And the banning of dancing in medieval churches.

The two mythical aspects around Neptune transits that I am picking out here are firstly the Maenads, who through surrender of the 'civilised' ego experience the ecstasy and secret knowledge of Dionysus's realm; and secondly the story of Pentheus, who symbolises the transformation that the resistant, controlling ego undergoes. Dionysus makes you mad, and leads you to a place where you are torn apart. But which is the real madness, Dionysus' realm, or that of the deluded ego which thinks it is in control? Neptune is the magical beast that we all have within. Or standing over our shoulder.

Chapter 15

The Post-War Neptune-Pluto Eras

Pluto takes about 100 years longer to go round the Sun than does Neptune, but its orbit is highly eccentric, meaning that it goes a lot faster through some signs than others. For about the last 65 years the two planets have been travelling at about the same speed through the sky, and this will continue through till the 2030s, when Neptune in Aries will at last start to pull clear of Pluto as he gradually brakes through Aquarius.

Coincidentally, Neptune and Pluto began travelling at the same speed when they were near enough 60 degrees, or exactly two signs, apart. Since then, therefore, they have always entered a new sign within a few years of each other – not long on their time scales.

Uranus, Neptune and Pluto are not visible to the naked eye and they therefore represent that which is unconscious, both personally and collectively. When one of them enters a new sign, humanity undergoes a shift, even a transformation, according to the nature of the outer planet and the sign it is in. It usually takes some years, however, for the planet to establish itself in the new sign, and possibly some years after that before we mere humans can look back and see what it was about.

The planets as gods (a modern, sometimes controversial, astrological identification) exist outside of time and space. The results of their actions, the past, present and future, are instantly clear to them. If we are intuitively gifted, then those patterns may be clear to us too, at least to some extent, maybe in flashes now and again. We, however, are creatures of clay, our journey is through time and space: those flashes can be helpful, but it is not our place to know the minds of the gods, to see too much of the deeper patterns of development that we are passing through individually and collectively, or else we would not be able to live them.

This is why full-time psychics and 'spiritual' teachers are sometimes a bit wonky (technical term), because they try to live too much in this intuitive dimension, they over-identify with it, at the expense of other aspects of being human.

Saturn is the planet that balances this out. He is the bridge between the inner and outer planets, he shows us how to be an ordinary physical human, yet also connected to the wider, deeper, more meaningful patterns that are also part of being human.

As astrologers, discovering the deeper patterns, the hidden meanings, behind existence is precisely what we are about. It needs, however, to be in a way that is physically lived – the astrology is a mere pointer. I said it is not our place to know the minds of the gods, but at the same time nothing is more important. It's a matter of how you go about it. If it emerges organically from the way you live, from attempting to understand your experience, then that is balanced, that is Saturn. If you grasp after it, or if you identify yourself as that sort of person, whether as bishop or mullah, shaman or astrologer (!), then that can often suggest an attempt to bypass the actual living of it.

Incidentally, some shamans and astrologers love to say how their path is not a religion or a belief system unlike, for example, Christianity. Stuff and nonsense! In my experience they are just as prone to religion as anyone else.

Anything can be a religion or not a religion. The essential point is whether your understanding comes out of your experience or from what someone else has said, whether on this plane or another one, and whether you can tell the difference. If you're religious, what some authority has said comes before your own experience. If you're the real deal, it's your own lived and considered experience that is the authority. Of course, everyone likes to think their understanding is autonomous, that they are their own authority. And there are degrees of it. But that sort of independence, which is an emotional as well as a cognitive quality, is rarer than one might think.

You can also be a one-person religion. Yes, it's your own thoughts, but along the line you've got rigid, you've turned what was originally a fresh insight into a stale dogma that you refer back to. It's hard not to do this to some extent if you're a teacher repeating the same stuff over and over, or an astrologer doing several readings a day.

Knowing the meaning of an outer planet transit to our chart is not easy, nor should it be. Astrology helps us see that there is meaning in what is happening, it is not just random, and it can even point us roughly in the direction of what it means. But it is just a map, sometimes brilliant and inspiring and mind-boggling, but still just a map. It is not a substitute for the actual exploration.

And it is the same with the meanings for the collective of the outer planet transits. Our lives are not just a personal journey. We are intimately tied in to where the collective is going, whether we like it or not. Getting some sort of separation, some sort of distance from the collective is necessary if we are to understand anything, but not in such a way that we can pretend to ourselves we are not part of it.

This is why mundane astrology – the astrology of the world, of countries, of collectives – is important. It tells us where the world is going, and it reminds us that we are part of it. We are not just our personal chart. We are also our personal chart in relation, for example, to the chart of the country we live in, and in relation to the charts of our parents and so on. The personal chart cannot be fully understood in isolation.

It is not easy to understand the meanings for the collective of an outer planet in a sign, particularly at the time. We may have flashes of insight, and certain events may have an obvious connection, but the wider understanding takes time and cultural awareness and probably a lot of plodding through historical data.

Neptune and Pluto have been entering new signs within a few years of each other for many decades now, and coincidentally Uranus has also been part of that process. This means that the ages we have been passing through have been quite clearly defined.

Between 1955 and 1956, Uranus began to move into Leo, Neptune into Scorpio and Pluto into Virgo. This process took a few more years to complete and establish itself, but all three outer planets moving into new signs suggests a clearly defined new era, which is indeed what happened in the 60s, as the West moved economically from the post-war effort to re-establish itself into years of boom, and socially and politically into a rejection of old values and all sorts of cultural awakenings.

Exactly how this played out in terms of planets and signs would be very complex to analyse. You could say, for example, that the previous Pluto in Leo period had awoken a sense of the importance of the individual, the power of individuality, and Uranus coming into Leo furthered that process – heightened selfishness as well as opposition to authority. Pluto in Virgo ushered in a period where we began to rely much more on high technology (Virgo), and could no longer survive (Pluto) without it.

Neptune describes the myths we live by collectively, the stories we tell ourselves (hence its connection to fashion), and this was the era when the Cold War reached its height; the Cuban missile crisis and its threat of nuclear war occurred under Neptune in Scorpio. The collective story (Neptune) we were living under was one of death and annihilation (Scorpio). It was also a period when fashion (Neptune) was used as an instrument of power (Scorpio) – the clothes and long hair of the 1960s counter-culture were a deliberate provocation of the establishment, a challenge to what men and women were supposed to look like. It was flower (Neptune) power (Scorpio).

All three planets came together as Uranus entered Virgo later in the 60s: you had the intense protest and revolutionary intent of the Uranus-Pluto conjunction, which was in turn sextile to Neptune in Scorpio, making protest in a way fashionable, and connecting it to the counter-culture.

The two most defining planets in this way at looking at our modern eras are Neptune and Pluto, being further out than Uranus and, for now, operating in tandem. With Pluto the emphasis is on the economy and the balance of power (Pluto is a god of wealth); and with Neptune the emphasis is on our underlying mythologies, fantasies and ideals, as well as the general mood.

The general post-war economic boom era lasted until 1970-71, when both planets again changed sign: Pluto into Libra, and Neptune into Sagittarius. As they established themselves over the next few years, so began the first recession since the war and the loss of the idealism of the sixties. In a way it was a balancing (Libra): the Arabs were asserting themselves economically, demanding a fair price for their oil; newly industrialised countries were competing with the West's metal industries; and the US had been running at a deficit, partly due to the Vietnam War.

Sagittarius is a sign of excess in either direction, so while there was a feeling of despondency around the hopes of the 60s, there was also glam rock and the age of the gurus (Sagittarius is also religion) – Rajneesh and his 93 Rolls Royce's.

In 1983-84, Neptune moved into Capricorn and Pluto into Scorpio. There was a new economic boom on the way, not unlike the recent one, in which materialism became sexy – Neptune in Capricorn, combined with the raw power of money, of the bankers – Pluto in Scorpio. After a short recession in the early 1990s, the stage was set by the prolonged action of this materialistic combination to create the longest economic boom since the 1960s.

Also, in the early 90s we had what must have been the biggest event of this Neptune-Pluto Age, which was the collapse of Communism and a shift in the world balance of power towards the US and the West in general. The suddenness with which the collapse happened and the move into a different future speaks of Uranus, which was conjunct Neptune and sextile Pluto. Neptune in Capricorn can be dissolution of governments, and the ease with which it happened is described by the sextile to Pluto, functioning powerfully in his own sign of Scorpio. Saturn also joined Neptune and Uranus in Capricorn at this time, making for an incredibly powerful triple conjunction, the sort of astrology that is needed to give birth to a whole new world order. Saturn ensures that the deeper collective currents of the outer planets manifest.

America emerged as the world's lone superpower under Pluto in Scorpio. America's Pluto, its raw power, is in late Capricorn in the 2nd house of wealth: Neptune conjoined, and Pluto sextiled the US Pluto during this period. Neptune and Pluto also made soft aspects to the US Neptune at 22 Virgo around this time, creating a new mythology for the nation, which 'lone superpower', in the context of the 'New World Order', certainly is.

Pluto had been moving at its fastest for some time now, faster than Neptune, putting it inside its orbit, which meant there were there years between Pluto moving into Sagittarius (1995) and Neptune moving into Aquarius (1998). The collective has a short memory, and the prolonged boom set up by Neptune and Pluto in the 80s/90s inevitably led to excess and the feeling (as in 1929) that somehow the rules had changed. The first excess was the dotcom bubble, brilliantly described by Neptune (fantasy) in Aquarius (internet) and Pluto in Sag (economic boom). Pluto doesn't find it easy to function well in Sagittarius, as he lives not just on Earth but below it, while Sagittarius, ruled as it is by the king of the gods, is the sign least concerned with earthly reality.

Pluto was being pulled along by his sextile to Neptune in Aquarius, another very unearthy combination, creating over time an economic boom so ungrounded and corrupt that it eventually broke the financial system in 2008/9. (During both the 1980s and the Noughties economic bubbles, Pluto was inside the orbit of Neptune, in a way making Neptune the more powerful influence, adding to the possibility that fantasy (Neptune) would have a stronger than usual influence over the economy (Pluto).)

At the same time, the new internet age motored along famously, with Neptune in Aquarius being empowered not just by his sextile to Pluto, but also by the mutual reception to Uranus in Pisces (Neptune rules Pisces, and Uranus Aquarius.) The internet does not have a material existence that you can easily point to, and it is only partly governed by economic factors, so the Neptune-Pluto combination worked in its favour rather than against it. In writing about the internet, I am not just pulling out a cultural factor that suits the astrology (which you can always do); rather I am writing about something which started to change and define the whole culture, and whose full significance is not yet clear.

And so, to the present. (NB This chapter was originally written in 2011. It is predictive about the years following, so I am leaving that in, and then updating to 2021 along the way.)

Pluto began to change sign from Sagittarius to Capricorn in 2008, and Neptune will start to change to Pisces in April 2011. Pluto's entry into Capricorn was economically dramatic, more than you'd expect from a planet that usually takes time to make his presence felt, his changes being deep. But as Pluto entered earthy, level-headed Capricorn (a good sign for Pluto), so too did the ruler of Capricorn, Saturn, begin to oppose Uranus, a periodic combination that is always dramatic and revolutionary.

And so, we have had the Great Recession – a measure of just how out of balance things had become economically under Pluto in Sag/Neptune in Aquarius. At the same time, the chart for Pluto's entry into Capricorn was quite favourable – Pluto in a stellium with benefics Jupiter and Venus, and trine to Capricorn's ruler, retrograde Saturn. There is stuff to sort out (retrograde Saturn), and it will take the time it takes (Capricorn/ Saturn). It is a fundamental restructuring (Pluto). So, it will take time. It may still get worse before it gets better. But this combination doesn't suggest the extreme of Depression.

I think the fundamental issue is that the West has been living beyond its means and has to cut back, and while it does so, China will become ever more powerful, leading to a major shift in the balance of power worldwide. There are no signs that the basic economic model is going to change (which the astrology could suggest) because for a while yet the resources – oil, minerals – will continue to be there, allowing us to continue as before.

Pluto in Capricorn is soon to work in tandem with Neptune in Pisces, and this is where we will have to speculate. I find it odd that Capricorn and Pisces sextile each other (a flowing aspect), because in their natures they are so different, even opposing. They are earth and water respectively, which is compatible, but Capricorn is so worldly and Pisces so unworldly that it is hard to see how they can get on healthily. You can, for example, just see Pisces capacity for empathy being put to ruthless and manipulative use by a Capricorn businessman. At best, though, Pisces can mellow a rigid and conservative Capricornian worldliness, and Capricorn can insist that Pisces puts its dreams into action. A successful artist, or a philanthropic businessman, could have this combination.

Neptune in Pisces is in its own sign, and as we saw with Pluto in its own sign in the 1980s, where the vulgar power of money was in the ascendant, it can bring out the worst. It could be a time when the collective tells fantastical stories about itself. I think China will be a match for America sooner than we realise, and how will America explain that to itself?

All countries think they are special, America more so than most. It is not a country to go into a quiet depression, like the UK did when it lost its Empire. The US is naïve and brash and extreme and proud. It will not say to itself that China is beating it in a fair fight. No, it will be seen as some sort of unfair conspiracy against America's rightful place in the world.

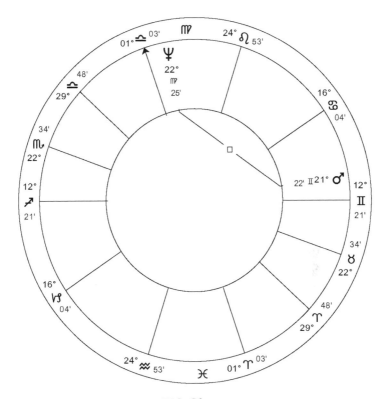

US Chart

With natal Neptune square to 7th house Mars, the US is used to creating myths (Neptune) about its foreign enemies (Mars in the 7th). These planets are at 21 Gemini and 22 Virgo respectively, which Neptune will begin to hard-aspect as it progresses through Pisces. Last time Neptune hard-aspected these two planets, in 1980/81, the country elected a cowboy actor for a President (Reagan) who promoted the myth of the Soviet Union as the Evil Empire. The next hard Neptune aspect will not be exact for another 10 years, but these transits can begin surprisingly early.

And what will America say to itself about the war it is losing against militant Islam? Who or what will America blame? In both US economic and foreign policy terms, there will be plenty of scope for Neptune's mythologising at its worst over the next 14 years. (Fast forward 10 years to 2021, when President Biden announced the withdrawal of troops from Afghanistan, where it had engaged in its longest ever war: the withdrawal amounted to an acceptance of defeat.)

For the West generally, putting Pluto and Neptune together, we are likely to see new mythologies created (Neptune in Pisces) to describe/compensate for the new economic realities (Pluto in Capricorn.) And for the new political realities, for money is power. China is currently arming itself at a frightening rate. And the West's implacable enemy, the militant Islam which arose so appropriately under Pluto in Sagittarius is, under Pluto in Capricorn, equally appropriately becoming the established power in many parts of the Middle and Near East, as well as southwards through Africa. And oil (Neptune) is at the heart of this struggle, particularly the West's dominance of those countries which supply it. Over the last 15 years, the US Progressed Saturn and Mars have both gone retrograde for the first time ever. America is on the retreat economically and militarily, and Europe with it.

Fast forward 10 years, and we can look back to 2016 as the year of Trump and Brexit. It was the year of backlash against globalisation (Pluto in Sagittarius) in favour of national sovereignty (Pluto in Capricorn – national boundaries). It was when Donald Trump wanted to 'make America great again' and the UK decided it wanted to stop sharing sovereignty with mainland Europe. One of the factors in both cases was the vote of those who had been left behind by globalisation, whose jobs had been exported to where the labour was cheapest, and who were now unemployed, and in some cases had been for generations. The UK acquired a new national mythology, in which it was no longer politically part of Europe. In the US, President Trump enacted a long overdue pushback against laissez-faire globalisation, when he insisted that China stop engaging in unfair trade practices. This was the good housekeeping that Pluto in Capricorn demanded, in the run-up to America's Pluto

Return in the sign of Capricorn. There was, however, little respect for truth in the pronouncements and tweets of Donald Trump, culminating in his assertion, on the basis of no evidence, that the 2020 election had been stolen. Millions of Americans were prepared to believe this lie, and it culminated in the storming of the Capitol in January 2021. Neptune and Pisces are known for lacking the usual boundaries; put the two of them together, and you get this kind of total fabrication and the mob consciousness that can go with it. Neptune was at the time squaring both the Sun and Moon of Donald Trump, the architect of the Capitol riot.

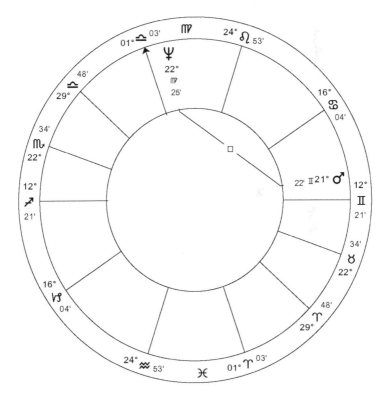

Neptune Enters Pisces

The chart for Neptune's 2011 Ingress into Pisces is striking: six planets in Aries, including a New Moon and a Mars-Uranus conjunction. We will really notice this transit: it is the start of something very, very new. Well, it would be, wouldn't it, because it will be the time when the West, dominant in the world for hundreds of years, first under Europe and then under its offspring America, will cease to be so dominant. The Far East will begin at least to equal it. And with economic influence (Pluto) comes cultural influence (Neptune). Look at what the West did with Christianity and Coca Cola. No doubt the turning point will, in retrospect, be seen as the time of the Uranus-Pluto conjunction which is seriously starting this year (2011), just as Neptune enters Pisces and asks us to re-formulate our mythologies, our stories about who we are.

As in the mid-1960s and early 1990s, Uranus entering the equation in 2011/12 is likely to bring a sudden surge forward in the underlying Neptune-Pluto story. In the Eurozone, for example, we could easily see the struggle with indebtedness spreading to a bigger economy such as Spain, which could be the last straw for the Euro: Europe as an economic bloc, as a potential united world power, could begin to unravel. (This in fact began with Brexit in 2016 and looks likely to unfold further in the mid-2020s as Neptune hard aspects the EU Angles.)

Chapter 16

Are We Fated?

We looked earlier at the way astrology works, at its essentially divinatory nature, and how, in some mysterious way, the universe seems to know who we are. By reading the chart, we can in some ways map out our future. Do we have choice, or are we fated?

The idea of fate can seem like an affront to our self-respect as human beings, to the idea that we have free will, that we make our own choices in life. It can seem like a throw-back to primitive superstition. This polarity is understandable when you look at our religious background with its all-powerful, all-determining God. We want none of that, and rightly so. Our destiny is no longer controlled by God but by ourselves, we have free will, and we are guided by reason. Or so we may think.

It's said that we become that which we oppose, and in our flight away from God and towards reason and science, we have created a determinism just as rigid: a universe governed by immutable physical laws, with human beings as just one more expression of those laws. And without even the divine element that God, for all his faults, brought.

But that determinism tends to be hidden because, at least in the West, in our day-to-day lives we do have the freedom to choose (up to a point) and to have opinions. We don't have to be on our guard, whatever people say about government snooping. Of course, we CAN be brainwashed by all sorts of factors, and many of us are in different ways, it seems to be part of how large societies work. But the point is we don't have to be, we have the option of thinking and acting independently without being sent to prison or burnt or beheaded.

These sorts of contradictions fascinate me. And I think they often arise because we think in rigid, literal, black-and-white terms. Life, hopefully, teaches us not to think like that. Education should also teach us not to, but I don't think it does, generally speaking, because it has its own agenda.

And so fate and free will can appear as irreconcilable opposites. I don't think I need to argue for free will, because it is self-evident. Or is it? In one sense it is self-evident, in that from moment to moment we choose our actions. The devil is in the word 'choose', and how much of 'us' is involved in that choice. We can truly and genuinely and sincerely think we are acting out of free will, and then one day we realise we've been living out a programme we were brought up to live, or reacting against it, which is sort of the same thing. The programming may have been making the choices to a greater extent than the little bit of consciousness we called our own. And that is fate, a certain kind of fate, masquerading as free will.

So, it's complicated. And often we wake up to free will through crises, which are fate in a rather different sense. As an astrologer, one sees this kind of fate all the time through the transits of the outer planets to the natal chart. A god enters the scene. He is wild and bad-mannered and can't be locked in his room, and a few years down the line you find you are a different person, maybe aware of the real reasons you've been like you are all these years.

These crises are, to a certain extent, predictable. They are writ, they are fate. They are part of the astrologer's box of magic tricks: what happened to you in some particular year, what major life change did you go through? And out it all comes, usually. Not always, because astrology isn't mechanical and people aren't mechanical.

Or take the financial crisis, the mother of all meltdowns, that began in 2008. Any half-way literate astrologer could see that with Uranus coming up to square Pluto at a degree that significantly impacted the charts of all the major powers, some sort of big crisis was on the way. Astrologers were in fact talking about it years in advance.

We'd have probably all had different ideas as to the nature of this crisis, although Uranus-Pluto has a way of being economics, so that would have been a reasonable guess.

It was the same with the Saturn-Pluto conjunction in Capricorn of January 2020: we all knew something very big was on the way, we just didn't know what. And then Covid happened.

So, you can see that the future was both writ and not writ on a collective scale.

It's mysterious. What is the chart if not our fate? But it is not set in stone. It is more like a set of stories that have their own flavours and lessons and turning points, and that can even to a great degree be predicted in advance. And these pre-writ stories are not a denial of our free will, but rather contain points at which events seem to have guided us to the possibility of an accession of free will.

The chart is not literal, it is a divinatory lens. It is objective, in that many astrologers would accurately see the same sort of meaning in a chart. It is not just a lens for the astrologer's personal dialogue with the gods, though it is that as well, which makes every reading unique and particular.

Through feeling and reading the relationship between Earth and the sky, astrology has over the millennia built a divinatory sea that anyone can tap into (another term for this is 'egregore'), a sea that points to our origins, in fact to the origins of everything, as lying behind the apparent material universe. For how else could we possibly know these things about people and world events from the chart? Certainly not from any physical cause.

As Wordsworth says in Intimations of Immortality:

"There was a time when meadow, grove, and stream,
The earth, and every common sight,
To me did seem

Apparell'd in celestial light,
The glory and the freshness of a dream...
Our birth is but a sleep and a forgetting:
The Soul that rises with us, our life's Star,
Hath had elsewhere its setting,
And cometh from afar"

I think this is the sort of context in which the fate element in astrology needs to be seen. Astrology gives us glimpses of the deeper stories behind our life, the intentions of the gods, if you like, the bigger cosmic picture behind who we think we are, that Aries has forgotten and that Pisces is privilege to, and that all the other signs are a gradual progression towards.

Fate in this sense is not something that can easily be put in rational, logical terms. Even free will cannot very easily be expressed in those terms, not when you view it as the urge to enlarge consciousness.

We may not be able to explain fate, but we ignore it at our peril. The ancient Greeks understood this well, though human rationality was given more power as time went on.

The ancient Greeks acknowledged the role of fate as a reality outside the individual that shaped and determined human life. In modern times, the concept of fate has developed the misty halo of romantic destiny, but for the ancient Greeks, fate represented a terrifying, unstoppable force.

And they were right. Cataclysmic natural events apart (which nowadays we are largely shielded from, we forget the raw power of nature), you see the suffering people go through because they don't know how to listen to themselves, the self being much larger than everyday consciousness and often how we have been taught to be. Life exacts its revenge, or tries to pressure us into submission. You get cancer, your wife leaves you, your kids disown you, you get fired, you lose your home, anything you try goes wrong, maybe you even die.

Sometimes a crow is just a crow, and sometimes it means something. Sometimes these things just happen. It is a basic mistake to think that outer events always mirror inner events. No, the whole point is that reading signs is an art, and knowing when a sign is a sign and when it isn't, is part of that art, and part of astrology's subtlety.

That larger self is just one way of putting it. It is the gods knocking at the door. It is life itself and its need to move on. It is the Unconscious trying to further the process of individuation.

Whatever it is, it is not necessarily 'nice'. Astrology in this auguristic sense disrupts our domestic sanitisations, the habitual and the safe, by revealing the intentions of the gods.

The ancient Greeks understood fate to be a dark god when resisted. Even, at times, when not resisted. The concept of fate brings us closer not to that which is 'nice' but to that which is real and necessary.

As science and its ordered universe has progressed and tightened over the last 200 years, so have the outer planets, reality as uncontrollable fate, emerged. Bernadette Brady, in her book *Cosmos, Chaosmos and Astrology* advances the notions of Cosmos and Chaosmos. Cosmos is the ordered universe. Chaosmos is that aspect of the universe, weather systems, for example, that do not obey the laws of predictable cause and effect and that science has had to find other ways of describing. Hence Chaos theory, and the Chaosmos, to which she proposes that astrology essentially belongs.

You could say that free will belongs to Cosmos and fate to Chaosmos. Not that it is a rigid distinction. Chaos theory seems to me to contain an inherent contradiction, in that is attempting to reduce to rational description that which defeats rationality. But at least it constitutes some kind of acknowledgement by science that there are aspects to reality that will forever be beyond its grasp. Quantum reality has similar implications. Chaosmos, however, is not merely the special case that science can't reduce to an equation: it is the larger reality within which the very specialised methods of modern science take their place. But people aren't always interested in philosophy, and why should they be? So these kinds of implications don't always filter through. All the same, fate as that larger reality beyond human control that needs respecting seems to be implied by both Chaos Theory and Quantum Theory. Chaosmos seems a very evocative term for it, that also has a measure of scientific respectability.

Free will can to some extent be explained in rational terms. Scientists can do brain studies on how we make decisions, for example. Free will is an idea. But fate in its deeper sense of the gods barging through our front door cannot be explained, merely described and evoked.

In 1996 I encountered the Norns in a book called *The Wisdom of the Wyrd* by Brian Bates. They are three women who live in a hall by a well at the foot of Yggdrasil, the World Tree of Norse Myth. They take care of Yggdrasil with water from the well and sand from around it. They and other Norns determine the destiny of new-born children.

The author called the Norns 'Daughters of the Night'. I knew nothing about these figures, yet the imagery stunned me. For weeks afterwards it was like I was left reeling whenever I thought of these Norns. Even now I sort of go weak at the knees.

I responded so strongly partly because Germanic/Norse myth is in me and probably in all northern Europeans. That is the strange thing about myths: we may not have heard them, but we recognise them all the same. *The Lord of the Rings* has that sort of quality, and it would, for Tolkien was deeply versed in European mythology.

My response was to an image of fate. But also, more than an image. These 'images' (which is what nowadays we reduce them to, like one more defined thing to have ideas about) are also beings, they are presences that we can experience. I have that with Pluto. I often feel his presence when I am writing.

And I don't think that is just a 'subjective' thing. These beings are real, they can be met and talked to. Yet they are also elusive, they do not just come at our bidding. And that is how I feel about the Norns. They belong to what Patrick Harpur calls 'Daimonic Reality'.

If I were southern European, I might well feel the same way about the Moirai, the Fates, the three women who in ancient Greece allotted the fate of everyone at birth. They each have a different function: one spins the thread of life onto her spindle, the other measures it, and the other cuts it: Clotho, Lachesis and Atropos.

The Norns and the Moirai suggest to me that in ancient times fate was understood and even feared as utterly real, yet it was not taken in the literal way that we think nowadays. For us, something is only real if it is literal, if it is 'out there' in a solid way and can be measured. From that point of view, fate can seem like a product of primitive ignorance. The modern perspective can seem to be above and beyond all that has come before, but I think that perspective is an anomaly, a peculiarity that will at some point change – though maybe not for a while yet – because imbalances are unstable and, on a collective level, eventually tip over into a different, maybe opposite, imbalance.

I think the Norns and the Moirai, understood in a non-literal way, bring us a long way from fate as a sort of primitive determinism, that we moderns with our understanding of the way the universe 'really' works can afford to look down on. I don't think the relationship between fate and free will can ever be pinned down. It is a dichotomy that is there for us to reflect on, to muse on, and in so doing to reach down below the surface of life and observe consciousness in its mystery and elusiveness.

Chapter 17

The Depth Psychology of Chiron

I occasionally try to do away with Chiron. He is, after all, only the size of the Isle of Wight. But he keeps coming back, one way or the other. So although I'm not going to give him planetary status, I will generally pay attention if he is aspecting something important in the chart. Like in my own case, conjunct the Sun and sextile the Moon.

But that still often leaves me stuck for something to say. Which 'bit' of us is he? It's not enough to say 'the wound' because many bits of us are problematic and painful. Besides which, Chiron was a wise teacher for the main part of his life, it was only later on that he got wounded by the poisoned arrow, and was in pain to such an extent that he tired of living. Catch: he was immortal. But he sorted that, giving up his immortality in exchange for Prometheus being released from his torment.

Both Saturn and Chiron have been described as bridges to the outer planets, and that seems a fairly sensible thing to say, given their positions in the solar system, on the boundary between the visible and invisible planets. It is the invisibility (to the naked eye) of Uranus, Neptune and Pluto that gives them a different character to the inner planets.

The way I'm thinking about Chiron at present is that he is the principle of the wound in the sense of that kind of difficulty and pain that can only be addressed by listening to the outer planets: he is precisely that principle you get in depth psychology that says that it is through our intractable, painful bits that we find our souls.

Imagine the outer planets as the molten core of Earth – uncontrollable, transformative and nuking everything in its path when it breaks through the surface crust. Chiron is that fissure deep underground, that fault line, through which the molten lava can erupt. And Saturn is the crust itself, the form of the earth, over which the lava flows. The outer planets are not always out of control and disruptive, particularly if we know how to listen to them. In this case Saturn is more like machinery erected at the surface to direct the raw power coming from below. An oil rig, something like that.

Chiron is this fissure deep underground. It cannot be sorted on its own terms, and it cannot be understood in terms of surface mechanics, earth movers and such like, ordinary psychology. No, for there is always this threat from below, or what appears as a threat. The threat that is actually our souls if we are willing to go there.

This is why Chiron often represents a part of life – depending on where he is in the chart – that doesn't work very well. You cannot patch him up, because there is always that roiling underneath. I think Chiron conjunct the Ascendant can be particularly difficult. The Asc is our basic ability to express who we are and make our lives work. With this placement you can bumble along in life with nothing quite working, nothing ever going anywhere, and that can go on for decades. And the problem is that you're trying to do 'normal', you're trying to live your life like everyone else does, but somehow your heart is not in it, and you feel inadequate because of that. But once you go bugger that, there's this thing I've always wanted to do, it's not going to earn me much probably and I don't know if I'll be any good at it but I'm going to do it, then your life can start to work properly – not in 'normal' terms, but in terms of you feeling there is something essential that is falling into place.

Chiron is a 'wound', but not an ordinary one. He only appears as a wound, and that's why it's said to be incurable, because you can't cure a wound that isn't a wound. What 'cures' it lies in making what is immortal in you mortal, just like Chiron himself did, giving earthly expression to that other drumbeat you've always heard.

The Chiron wound can make you feel like you don't want to go on living, just like Chiron the centaur felt. But I think it's a case of not wanting to live on particular terms, not if life has to be like this.

In 1999 I took ayahuasca a couple of times in the Amazon jungle, and it made me aware of what I think was Chiron. It was a sense of deep, existential pain, which I would experience from time to time anyway, but it became clear that that pain was what grounded me, connected me to the earth, it had a sort of weight to it. And then I became aware that I learnt from it, it was an ongoing source of learning. And it wasn't something that could be put into words and certainly wasn't to be psychoanalysed. It was uncomfortable, but very creative, and not to be ignored.

Previous to that, in the early 90s, I had driven myself into a corner by pressurising myself to 'achieve'. And I ended up realising, like Chiron, that I didn't want to live on those terms, I didn't have a will to live if it meant living like that. I didn't feel depressed or suicidal or anything, I just knew that I had to find a different way of being. This was as transiting Pluto was squaring my natal Sun-Chiron. And it was, appropriately, to do with work, my Sun-Chiron being in the 6th house. So, I've had to spend years undoing the notion of 'achievement' in the way I work, or pushing and pressurising myself. That sort of self-pressuring may work for some people, it's quite 'normal' in a way, but it ain't going to work if Chiron is involved in the 6th House. It means I 'do' less, but what I end up doing has a quality that it never had previously.

Chiron has this unconventional, outsider, even scapehorse quality to him. If Chiron doesn't aspect anything major in your chart, you may be able to ignore him. But if he, for example, conjoins your MC then you probably have something important to do in the world, and the 'career' aspect of your life will never feel right as long as you judge yourself in conventional terms.

You need to do what the outer planets want you to do, and that can take a long time to come to fruition – it's not like deciding to become a plumber and getting on with it. What you do may not have a name.

Gordon Brown, the UK Prime Minister from 2007-10, has Chiron conjunct MC. Everyone knew he wasn't Prime Minister material, but he was determined to get the top job, and it never worked very well for him. But he also has another side to him, he is a feelingful guy, he wants to be of help. He doesn't preen himself; he has more humility than say Tony Blair (another Chiron MC man). But because he wouldn't, couldn't listen to his Chiron, he ended up in a conventional job that didn't seem to suit him. And the same with Blair, look how hated he became. You could say his faith foundation, subsequent to being PM, is an attempt to get it right with Chiron. And George W Bush – Moon conjunct Chiron, Sun square Chiron: the debate about him has not been whether or not he was a bad President, but whether he was the worst or only second worst!

So, I think Chiron can be a sort of curse if you haven't got the wherewithal to step outside of conventional life and its expectations and judgements – and that can be a really difficult call for many people – and let the outer planets decide how you're going to live.

Chapter 18

The Second Half of Life

"I have treated many hundreds of patients. Among those in the second half of life – that is to say, over 35 – there has not been one whose problem in the last resort was not that of finding a religious outlook on life. It is safe to say that every one of them fell ill because he had lost that which the living religions of every age have given their followers, and none of them has really been healed who did not regain his religious outlook." – Carl Jung

This process of finding a 'religious' outlook in the second half of life is described by the series of outer planet transits that everyone has in their forties. It is a time when – archetypally – we move from the received and extraverted values of society to listening to the voice within. Of course, some of us may have done that from a much younger age, but there is usually still a struggle between who we feel we are expected to be, and the direction in which that mysterious voice within is taking us. I recommend *The Middle Passage* by James Hollis, a Jungian analyst, for an in-depth exploration of this theme.

This period begins with Uranus opposition Uranus in the early forties, which has the function of breaking up the landscape of the received values that have hitherto given us our sense of acceptance and identity, and opening up fissures, abysses that may be terrifying to peer into, but which reveal the voice of our deeper self that has always been there.

Now the picture gets confusing as to what happens when. But it is often a long, confusing period anyway, because the paradigm shift, the re-orientation is so radical. For many of us, the period will have begun with Pluto square Pluto rather than the Uranus Opposition, because of Pluto's elliptical orbit;

for anyone born now, the Pluto square will occur after the other transits that happen in this period: Neptune square Neptune and Saturn opposition Saturn. It finishes, aged 50, with the Chiron Return.

It is best to see this period as a bunch of influences, and create a story dependent on the order in which they occurred for you. And put it all together as a Creation Myth, much as we can see the Big Bang as a creation myth described by the outer planets: Uranus lit the touch paper for this utterly unpredictable event, of everything suddenly coming out of nothing; Pluto was the enormous creative power in that tiny singularity; Neptune was the Primordial Imagination that contained the vision of a Universe; and Saturn put all the pieces together.

We can see all these influences running alongside each other as we are born into the second half of life. Pluto square Pluto will be the time when we are made an offer we cannot refuse, of that seed of new and more authentic life that is trying to push through, and which can make us ill if we deny it; Neptune square Neptune is the whisper, the longing for the life we have always secretly wanted to lead, the magical thread of Self that has followed us since childhood; and Saturn opposite Saturn is a re-assessment in this reality of what has value for us, the perhaps painful realisation that what we had strived for over a long period now means little to us.

As we approach 50, the Chiron Return presents itself. Chiron, as the bridge to the outer planets, is telling us to listen to their drumbeat from now on, or our life will not work, it will be 'wounded'. Chiron is also a teacher, and having been through this long initiation, we will have learnt something important that we can impart.

Chapter 19

Astrology, Psychotherapy and Ritual Space

Astrology, in my view, is essentially divinatory. It is not a 'science' in the sense of its statements being reducible to testable rules. The rules – the chart itself and its formal meanings – provide a framework for this other thing that we do. They even carry a bit of the magic of the divinatory process; something has rubbed off on them over the centuries. But only a bit. Push the 'rules' too far, subject them to too much statistical testing, and they tend to break down.

The 'rules' are essentially ceremony, the forms that guide the astrologer into the liminal space where real astrology, divination, takes place. We've probably all experienced this at the start of a reading: the astrologer is running through the formal meanings of some of the planets in their signs and aspects, but already the divination is there in the form of which part of the chart the astrologer has homed in on. Or in which of the wide range of possible meanings the astrologer is applying.

You get ceremony at the start of any magical, divinatory or healing process. Psychotherapy is magical healing half-masked as science. The procedures around it are a sort of ritual – meeting at the same time, sitting opposite one another in chairs, and the personal 'boundary' that the therapist maintains, which is there in order to be a vessel for the spirits, like a priest running a service, or a high priestess invoking Isis. (This role can be enhanced by the sense of lineage and transmission going back to the founders of psychotherapy – it's something you get in many religions.)

That is what Freud was really doing when he had his patients on a couch, unable to even see him: it was powerful magic, rather than the attempt at scientific 'objectivity' that it would seem to be.

Unfortunately, that impersonal magical 'boundary' has resulted in personal disclosure on the part of the therapist becoming a taboo, so that even when it would be highly appropriate, the psychotherapist is often reluctant to bring in personal experience. I think this taboo has arisen through the cultural need to appear 'scientific' – or maybe 'professional' – which as I say obscures the real meaning of the magical boundary. And also, if we are honest, to keep it 'safe' for the therapist: the boundaries end up serving the therapist rather than the client.

I think that the liminal space, in which the ordinary social rules are relaxed, allowing something 'other' to come in, is common to both astrology and psychotherapy at their best. The ceremonies are different, but the divinatory principle is the same. I could argue that the astrological ceremonies are more developed and efficacious than those of psychotherapy, which to some extent likes to imagine itself a science, and so can be reluctant to admit, let alone develop, its ritualistic aspect. But even astrologers are on the defensive about their own magical roots, and some like to imagine there is some scientific, testable basis to their craft, despite the firm evidence to the contrary. (See *The Moment of Astrology* by Geoffrey Cornelius.)

That 'liminal space', you could argue, takes place at the border between the Conscious and Unconscious minds. I think we all have an ability to go there. The 'Unconscious' feeds us: another word for it is simply 'life'. And if you are functioning as some sort of healer or mentor, then you have a gift – that usually requires training – for going to that place. Ordinary life often requires that our gaze is directed outwards, and indeed that is often where people feel most comfortable.

That other natural function, of consulting life within, can get projected onto healers and therapists as a special gift – which they may well have – but the point is we all have it, it is natural. And it involves the principle of finding our own answers in a culture that too readily supplies them. And an important function of the healer/therapist/astrologer is to motivate that sort of enquiry. When people want 'a reading' from me, I sometimes do a double-take, because of the way it can be couched. Almost as through the other person wants just to listen to what I have to say about their chart. I have occasionally had this sort of flavour even when experienced astrologers have asked me for 'a reading'. Whereas I like to see a 'reading' mainly as a platform for the other person's self-enquiry, actively promoted by myself, and with hopefully a measure of insight from myself, particularly as the reading progresses. Sure, it will start out with mainly me doing the talking, as I let the chart speak to me. But then it has to land, it needs to promote an engagement, a response, from the client.

I think there is an issue around the cultural baggage that astrology carries. You go to an astrologer for answers, particularly about the future: that is the sort of archetype that is in the culture, and that as astrologers we need to be aware of and to resist. The function of the oracle at Delphi was to help people to live well, rather than tell them what was going to happen, and I think that also needs to be our function. I think astrology has probably taken a few wrong turns down the centuries, but we are fortunate enough to live in a time when tradition can be questioned. Mistakes can be old and venerable.

Back to liminality. In our culture, alcohol has this function on a social level. We are allowed to be and to behave in ways that are normally proscribed, but even this relaxation has its limits. Parties and celebrations, which usually involve alcohol, also have this liminal function. In this place, we are allowing more of life in.

Amongst the Chippewa-Cree Indians, human consciousness is seen as a tiny thing within the context of the vast consciousness of the universe. How, by implication, with our tiny minds, can we understand more than a sliver of all-that-is? It is the same principle, but modernised, with the idea of the Conscious and the Unconscious (in the broader, Jungian sense). The conscious mind is likened to the tip of the iceberg above the surface of the ocean, with the great majority being underwater. But even that does not do it justice, for the conscious, individual mind is finite, whereas the Unconscious is infinite. So, in that liminal space as healer/astrologer, we go to that boundary of finite Consciousness and infinite Unconscious, hopefully the other person is there too, and we listen to what that infinite ocean has to say.

Our modern, scientific worldview often denies this much bigger source: the hubris of science is that the human mind is God, it can understand all. And so life itself gets pushed out. But, because life cannot be truly pushed out, it returns in another form. In our quest to understand the cosmos, we have arrived at the point where, over the last 20 years or so, the universe is seen as being made up of 95% dark energy and dark matter: 'stuff' that has to be there for theoretical reasons but which is undetectable! So again, we are back to the principle of the tiny human mind and the vast unknowable universe – except in this case, there is a degree of demonization, in that the universe is seen as largely cold and indifferent rather than life enhancing.

It is interesting that the internet also seems to be taking on this mythological, asymmetrical polarity: the web most of us know is very small compared to the so-called 'deep web'. So that even sat at our computer, the new 'reality', there is something much bigger behind it. And again, there is a degree of demonization: the deep web is not just mountains of academic papers, but a vast culture of harmful activity – the 'dark web' – largely beyond cultural control.

You could argue that computerised reality shuts out important aspects of life, particularly real engagement with real people, and easily becomes a way of shutting ourselves down. And, thinking mythologically, that throws up a shadow, the dark web.

I think this liminal, divinatory space is where we are most

human: it requires all our faculties of awareness, both of ourselves and of the people around us, but also of the source of life within that is, in a way, beyond analysis. There has always been a human tendency to think we know more than we do. Wisahitsa, a trickster character in some of the American Indian stories, is always running into trouble because he thinks he knows more than he does. The ancient Greeks were aware of it through the idea of hubris, thinking you are a god. And the modern dazzling success of science and technology and economic prosperity has caused perhaps an unprecedented level of thinking-we-know-it.

But that awareness of an ocean that is inherently beyond us and that nourishes us, the Pisces principle, is never far away. Perhaps that is one of the main things that astrology has to offer nowadays. We get too easily caught up in trying to defend our craft on a technical level. Protesting to the media, for example, that there are really only 12 signs and not 13, gives the public the impression that there is something real and literal about these signs. I say OK, respect the tradition, ceremonial forms matter, they give power. But really astrology is about using those forms to go to a place within where life is and where wisdom is and where also we find the limits of what we can understand. It is a magical place within that has been forgotten and, in my view, that is what astrology is really about. Rather like alchemy.

Astrology shouldn't be mistaken for its outward forms – in a way, people are right to laugh at them if they are presented as literally true. I think that on a popular level astrology needs to be reinvented as essentially an inner tradition, and as ceremony that takes us there.

Chapter 20

In Defence of the 13th Sign

The idea of the 13th sign puts many astrologers up in arms, and it may seem I am being merely provocative in defending it. The reason I am doing so, however, is because the 13th sign works, and this fact illuminates the real nature of astrology as being essentially divinatory, rather than a system with rules.

In the late 70s, someone mentioned to me that there used to be a 13th sign of the zodiac and that it had something to do with a spider. I was intrigued. I had a strong feeling for astrology, but I knew nothing about it (which is probably why I was better then at guessing people's star signs than I am now.)

I never followed up on the 13th sign, but I did hear it mentioned from time to time. It was only later, when I saw a piece on Facebook protesting (quite rightly) at the BBC's inaccurate presentation of astrology that I found out properly about this mysterious sign, Ophiuchus.

From the point of view of traditional astrology, the 13th sign is a piece of nonsense, invented in about 1970. What happened was that in 1930 the astronomers redefined the boundaries of the constellations so that Ophiuchus was now behind the Sun from Dec 1 to Dec 18 each year.

From there it was a short step to someone saying, well in that case it is a zodiac sign, because that is how zodiac signs are defined: they are the constellations on the Sun's path through the sky (the ecliptic).

Except that the signs aren't defined that way, not any more. Originally, the signs would have been based around the constellations on the ecliptic. But then they got tidied up into 30 degrees each (which of course they aren't) and since that time, due to precession, they have drifted 23 degrees off that original alignment.

The signs are a fiction, as they have nothing to do with the stars anymore (though I don't think the public is usually aware of that!) They are simply a way we have of dividing space into 12 segments, based around the seasons instead of the stars. So that Aries always begins at the spring equinox. Whereas in India, where they take precession into account, Aries now begins in mid-April.

Incidentally, it may seem to some that Vedic astrology, which takes precession into account, must therefore be more accurate than western astrology. The answer to that is that both use 30 degrees for each sign, and that is an artifice. So, in neither tradition do our charts reflect accurately what is happening in the sky. I would argue, if anything, that with western astrology, it is clearer that, taken literally, it is all a piece of nonsense, and therefore clearer that astrology is essentially divinatory rather than some kind of science.

Back to Ophiuchus, it makes no sense to call it a sign, because it is a constellation, and the constellations are not the signs. If we were to incorporate it, it would make a mess of all the symmetry and symbolism that comes with having 12 signs.

And yet…. The 13th sign clearly has popular appeal, and it doesn't look like it's about to go away, especially with the BBC promoting it! One of the myths surrounding it is that 2000 years ago it was a zodiac sign (not true), and the astrologers of the time excluded it (another piece of nonsense). That adds to its mystery, so when modern astrologers also shut it out, that almost adds to the mystique. An excluded, hidden part of the psyche.

I would argue that a tradition needs to respond to popular appeal if it wants to stay alive. Much as the Church did in the 10th century, when the Pope began canonising saints, which up till then had just been a local, popular practice. There's nothing about canonising saints in the Bible, and no doubt some theologians dismissed it as doctrinal nonsense, and they would have been right. But if something has popular appeal, you can always adjust the doctrine.

And maybe astrologers also need to look at their criteria for incorporating change. When a new planet is discovered by astronomers, we accept it, and we accept the mythology around the name of the planet, even though the name is decided upon by astronomers. And astronomers are not people we generally think of as sympathetic to astrology. Yet when people who *are* sympathetic to astrology – a large section of the public – run with a new piece of mythology that has no basis in doctrine, we are quick to dismiss it. Our instinct seems to be not to adapt. Maybe we are too intellectual, so that astronomers get taken seriously where popular feeling does not?

But does the 13th sign really have no basis in astrological theory? Do we, in other words, over-egg the difference between signs and constellations? Because the origin of the signs was indeed the constellations, before the systematisers came along and tidied it all up.

Geometrically/astronomically, the signs and constellations are not the same. But mythologically, they are closely related. The signs are fundamentally mythological, they tell us ancient stories about ourselves, that is part of their deep appeal, and they are the same myths as the constellations associated with them.

So, if a constellation is reconfigured so that it is, to some extent, on the ecliptic – as in the case of Ophiuchus – then I think it is, in a way, true to say that it becomes part of the zodiac, because the zodiac's foundations are those constellations on the ecliptic.

That, if you like, is my theoretical case for the 13th sign. And my practical case is that it has popular appeal – in other words, it has found its way in, at least to some extent, whether we like it or not, and however much we may huff and puff about doctrinal incorrectness. Much as the outer planets and their mythologies have found their way in through astronomy, so has the 13th sign found its way in through its popular appeal. Not only do we need our public, but there can be a wisdom in that popular feeling, even if it's based on what we see as muddled thinking, and so I think it needs paying attention to.

So, what are we going to do with Ophiuchus? Astrology is a flexible tradition, and in its modern form we find room for extra planets, asteroids and the Galactic Centre along with imaginary bodies such as Vulcan and the Dark Moon.

But I don't think we can just pat Ophiuchus on the head and give him a new and minor category and then quietly ignore him, while congratulating ourselves on being broad-minded. He has come in as a sign of the zodiac, and therefore needs to be treated as such. The way he has come in is part of the sign's divinatory qualities, along with the mythology behind Ophiuchus.

I don't say we have to change the zodiac to incorporate him (though maybe we could?) No, we can keep the same zodiac, but then – if we want – add in to our reading any planets in that sign, which extends from about 8 to 26 Sagittarius (yes, the Galactic Centre at 26 Sag harbours the dark secret of Ophiuchus) and which is now also 0 to 18 Ophiuchus.

Ophiuchus is a man grappling with a serpent, the only sign to contain both man and beast. The mid-point of early Aquarius and early Scorpio is in Ophiuchus – the man and the serpent, he resolves these two signs.

The 1st century Roman poet Manilius describes the constellation thus (from Wikipedia):

"Ophiuchus holds apart the serpent which with its mighty spirals and twisted body encircles his own, so that he may untie its knots and back that winds in loops. But, bending its supple neck, the serpent looks back and returns: and the other's hands slide over the loosened coils. The struggle will last forever, since they wage it on level terms with equal powers."

It is powerful imagery. Man grappling with his demons, but they are equals, he does not slay them like St George, but meets them with a respect which is mutual. Aquarius meets Scorpio: the archetypal human meets the archetypal demon.

It seems that in modern times, this principle is having to force its way in, if the response of the astrological world to Ophiuchus is anything to go by. We live in an age of ideas, of scientific and technological progress (Aquarius) and the dark side of that (Scorpio) is all around us in environmental degradation, terrible weapons and an alienation from the rhythms of nature. Aquarius here is also the astrologers with their beautiful, human-made systems; and Scorpio is the popular feeling that doesn't always have much regard for such systems, that just likes a good story, even if it's not true. It's as if through Ophiuchus, that principle of integration of man and beast, human consciousness and its origins, is wanting to make a new synthesis between technological man and nature.

Later in his poem, Manilius describes the astrological influence of Ophiuchus, when the constellation is in its rising phase, as one which offers affinity with snakes and protection from poisons, saying:

"he renders the forms of snakes innocuous to those born under him. They will receive snakes into the folds of their flowing robes, and will exchange kisses with these poisonous monsters and suffer no harm"

This seems to suggest a healing quality. For the Romans, the figure in Ophiuchus was Asclepius, the Healer. And again, from Wikipedia:

"To the ancient Greeks, the constellation represented the god Apollo struggling with a huge snake that guarded the Oracle of Delphi"

This brings us back to astrology: the use of reason to create a system (Apollo) and the divinatory power that system was built to serve (the Oracle); the tension, hopefully creative, that you get between the two, that one seems to get in any spiritual tradition: the direct experience of the mystic, and the wisdom of the book.

But what about some divination? After all, the above is no use if Ophiuchus does not have divinatory validity. And I thought the quality I want to look for is a struggle with demons as characterising the life of someone with Sun in Ophiuchus, and that I'd see who I had on my personal list of famous people in my astrology programme. There were just two of them, Jim Morrison (of the Doors) and the painter Edvard Munch.

Jim Morrison is well known for his losing battle with his own demons, resulting in his death, aged 27, of a heroin overdose. And Munch is known to all of us as the painter of *The Scream*, portraying the existential anxieties of modern people. That was enough for me. This thing works. I don't test divination with statistics, because it doesn't work that way. I test it with what immediately presents itself to me, and that was a double hit. That was the universe telling me I was onto something.

If you have substantial personal placements in Ophiuchus, your life is likely to be characterised more than most by a struggle with demons, which you may at times be losing (Morrison), or which you may turn into art for the collective (Munch); and whose wider context is the archetypal struggle (leading hopefully to synthesis) between humans and nature, a struggle that is particularly pressing right now as Ophiuchus pushes himself into view from the left field.

The fact that Ophiuchus as a sign of the zodiac has popular appeal, but is ridiculed by many astrologers, maybe suggests an imbalance between the intricate and beautiful astrological system that has developed over two millennia, and the raw divinatory power that system was built to serve.

Chapter 21

The Geography of the Underworld

In 2006 Pluto was demoted from planet to dwarf planet. I wrote at the time that it said something about our relation to the Underworld that we would do such a thing. I am, however, now more forgiving of the astronomers, because seven years later they named two more Moons of Pluto on the principle that the names, like the previous three, had to be mythologically related to Pluto. There are now five known Moons: Charon, Nix, Hydra, Kerberos, and Styx. So, while on the one hand we seem to have given the Underworld less significance, on the other hand we are now giving it more complexity, deliberately so. It feels like it is being honoured.

There was an online poll for the new names called Pluto Rocks! and the winning submission was Vulcan, sponsored by William Shatner (of Star Trek). It was, however, rejected by the committee on the grounds of not being related to the mythology of Pluto. A Vulcan in Star Trek mythology, of course, is a purely logical being, and the whole point about Pluto is that he disrupts our idealisation of reason, which can make us think we are masters of the universe; he insists that our loyalty should be to life itself rather than to our theories about it. The astronomers, whether they knew it or not, made a powerful archetypal statement.

Two years after Pluto was demoted, we experienced the biggest economic crash any of us remember – by some measures, like over-borrowing by banks and the time taken for the economy to start to recover, it has been bigger than the thirties. Pluto as a god of riches is associated with the economy. (Uranus in hard aspect to Pluto usually creates recessions.) After five years of this deep recession, we seemed to start honouring the underworld again, that place that brings us down to earth by destroying hubris, and the western economy seemed at last to be starting to recover.

This connection of the demotion of Pluto to the Great Recession may seem whimsical, to be stretching it, but I'd say as an astrologer that it is a matter of how seriously we take these powers. For an ancient Greek Tragedian, it might seem a simple matter of cause and effect.

What is this Underworld that Pluto rules? For the ancient Greeks, it was the place you went to after you died. For us astrologers, it is a psychological place or state.

Hades is the Greek for Pluto, as well as the name for the Underworld itself, Pluto's realm: I shall be using the terms Hades, Pluto and the Underworld somewhat interchangeably.

For the ancient Greeks, the Underworld was literally out there, invisible to us living humans, and located at the ends of the oceans or beneath the depths of the earth. I suspect it wasn't a belief held as rigidly, say, as the medieval Christian heaven and hell. Or as rigidly in the opposition direction as a modern who might say it is 'only' a psychological state and of course the underworld doesn't exist 'out there'.

I think the sense of 'in here' and 'out there' is a construct of the brain, and therefore not to be treated as a rigid distinction. When I die, I want a coin put in my mouth to pay the ferryman (Charon) to carry me across the Styx – or is it the Acheron – into Hades. As an astrologer, it makes perfect sense for me to feel like that, given that the Greek Lord of the Underworld is a major part of my cosmology.

For me, the Underworld is both within and without, in the same way that the gods/planets are both. I think that an ancient Greek would have experienced the gods with their demands as 'out there', while not at the same time experiencing any loss of personal freedom and choice. (Unlike the Christian experience at its worst with its rigid god.) It is like Jung said, that free will is the freedom to do what you have to do. That sums it up nicely for a modern.

When the planet known as Pluto was discovered and named after the Greek Lord of the Underworld – or, strictly speaking, the Roman god – I think that legitimised for astrologers the internalisation of the Underworld. It meant we could use the Underworld to describe that place we go to when we undergo a psychological death. And that would include anything that threatens the security of the personality we have built up, such as taboo areas. Things we feel we are not 'allowed' to be.

In the same way that the Underworld is deep below the earth, so is our personal Underworld deep within – and it is not just personal, it is collective. The Underworld is what we encounter when it is time to change, and it is life itself that brings that about. It is fundamental to life that it keeps changing, unfolding, moving on to the next stage. We see that in the natural world, and it is the same for human consciousness. When we resist it, illness often results.

So, another word for the Underworld, in a way, is life. The life force deep within that is beyond our personal planning and control, and that does not belong to us, we belong to it, and it is in this sense that the Underworld is collective.

I think that the discovery of Pluto has changed the metaphysics of astrology, which is itself a part of the western esoteric tradition that can be traced back to the Hellenistic culture of late antiquity, with its mixture of Greek philosophy and indigenous religious traditions. Here we find Platonism, which:

"focused on the attainment of a salvational gnosis ('knowledge') by which the human soul could be liberated from its material entanglement and regain its unity with the divine Mind."

From *Western Esotericism: A Guide for the Perplexed* by Wouter J. Hanegraaff. I think a better book is *The Elixir and the Stone* by Michael Baigent and Richard Leigh. It's a history of the western magical tradition, scholarly yet readable. It does, however, set the power of Renaissance magic above the magical abilities of earlier, indigenous peoples, and I think they have that wrong.

But there we have it: gnosis is attained through liberation from 'material entanglement.' The worldview implied by Pluto is the opposite of this. Pluto takes us deep within to a place where the body and all aspects of the psyche are sacred. Where the psyche and the body are both the expression of the same life-force, which is the same force that powers the universe.

Our task is not to free ourselves from material entanglement – with all the renunciation and suppression of desire that go with that – but to honour the life that flows through us and to experience the beauty and the sweetness of life. The Underworld is not just a dark place: it contains, for example, the Elysian fields.

Pluto and his Underworld are there to return us, after 1000 years of a relegation, even demonization, of the body and materiality, whether through mainstream or esoteric religion, to a more balanced, natural humanity.

Indigenous spirituality doesn't have this renunciative flavour at all, wherever you look. And that says to me that this deeper experience of life through the body and nature is what is natural to people, and that the ideal of freedom from material entanglement is a corruption.

The Underworld is a place of authenticity, of wholeness, where we are asked to acknowledge and honour the whole of ourselves. Maybe collectively as astrologers we have not asked ourselves rigorously enough what our philosophy is. Are we fully a part of the western esoteric tradition, or do we need to reject a central plank of that tradition? In a way Pluto makes astrology 'shamanic': a religion of 'this world' inhabited by spirits, by gods such as Pluto and Mercury for whom we are the mediators.

I began this chapter with the information that astronomers

have named Pluto's Moons after different Underworld figures. Maybe it is time to take a look at the structure of the Underworld, to understand its complexity.

It is easy to have a vague idea of the Underworld as a slightly dark place where we are dismembered and put back together under Pluto (and other) transits, and leave it at that. And it works. But maybe that's not enough.

At the same time, the Greek Mythology is only of limited help. The planets are named after Greek/Roman gods, but when you look into the stories behind them, there is not necessarily a lot to go on. There is virtually nothing in Greek mythology, for example, about the Moon, certainly not in our modern-day astrological understanding of her. Or Neptune – what there is about him bears very little resemblance to the astrological Neptune.

And philosophically, as I said earlier, our notion of Pluto is taking us away from a notion of progress in consciousness that involves a 'liberation' from the body.

I'm not quite sure where that leaves us. But it does in a way free us from the past. It is important to know the past, but we are not bound by it. At the same time, we need myths – what else is astrology but the intersection between timeless stories and personal lives? – and I think we can feel free to draw on whatever myths, from any part of the world, that illuminate our astrological symbols. We can look, for example, to the Norse tradition in which Odin hung himself upside down from the world tree without food or water for nine days in order to gain wisdom. That seems to have elements of both Pluto and Neptune transits.

I like to think of astrology as I like I think of all spiritual traditions, as a hodgepodge that has built up over the centuries, containing both gold and dross, even though we may sometimes feel tempted to search for some kind of pure origin or solid foundation.

While Greek Mythology may be a good starting point for our modern understanding of the Underworld, I don't think we should assume it will be sufficient. At the same time, there is some quite good stuff there. The Underworld is structured, it has geography. There are five rivers associated with it, as well as Tartarus, the Fields of Punishment, the Asphodel Meadows, the Elysian Fields and the Isles of the Blessed.

There are also various figures associated with the Underworld: Pluto/Hades, of course, who is King; his wife Persephone; the Erinyes, Hermes, Minos, Charon and Kerberos. The Hydra guarded an undersea entrance to the Underworld and Nix (the other Moon) is not strictly Underworld either, but she is the mother of Charon, is the goddess of darkness and night and was there near the beginning of creation. So, I think we have to give her honorary membership!

I'm not going to attempt an exhaustive correspondence between the Greek Underworld, and what we understand of Pluto/Scorpio astrologically. But we can draw quite a lot from a consideration of the figures and geography.

First of all, there is the myth of the abduction of Persephone, which is one of the myths that every astrologer knows, along with the story of Chiron. Persephone was the daughter of Demeter, a nature goddess, and Pluto abducted her into his Underworld, raped her (in some accounts) and married her. Demeter spent ages looking for her and in her despair the world turned to winter. Eventually she found her, but Pluto would only let her back for six months of the year, which is summer, while the six months of winter, when Demeter mourns, is when her daughter is back with her husband. (Demeter/Persephone/Hades in the ancient Greek pantheon are Ceres/Proserpina/Pluto in the Roman pantheon: I have conflated them here.)

So, there is a big theme here, almost like the Fall from primordial innocence of both Demeter and Persephone, that at the same time allows life to change, to progress. Persephone grows up, she becomes a wife, and it happens by force – life has to move on, and if we don't want to, well it will happen anyway. It's not really force; it is just natural progression – it is just experienced as such when we resist it. And through this Fall also comes the seasons – the continual death and renewal that is life, and you can't have one without the other. Every stage of life, however well-balanced and stable and happy, eventually tips over into a new stage, and for that to happen the old has to go. There may be a bleak winter stage that is more appearance than reality, for life is continuing in another form: it has withdrawn into the trunk and roots where it is being re-imagined, re-dreamed. The astrologer's job when someone is undergoing a major Pluto transit is often to point this out, to encourage them to tune in to the inner alchemy that is occurring outside of conscious control.

People with a strongly Plutonian/Scorpionic chart experience this Underworld continually. For them it is not a separate part of life like a hospital, but an integral part of things: Plutonians are always tuned in to this more basic, survival, life-as-it-is aspect, they are not persuaded out of it by mere ideas and social norms.

Even then they may have to start off by learning this about themselves. For someone unused to it, a major Pluto transit can be a traumatic experience.

Part of this is the initial death, perhaps the loss of home or health or relatives or career – all these can be Pluto's work. This can be the price we have to pay to enter his transforming world; this is the coin we give to the ferryman Charon. There is always a price.

Hermes/Mercury may have brought us to the gates of the Underworld in the first place. He is the messenger of the gods: Pluto has called us, and Hermes persuades us to come. He may even trick us into coming. I had a dream in 1996 telling me what to do next with my life, so I did it, and quite quickly it all became successful yet very painful and conflicted. My whole life changed, I started over. At the time, Pluto was between squaring my Sun and conjoining my IC, and Uranus – another trickster – was on his way to conjoin my Mercury.

Cerberus or Kerberos is the three-headed hell hound whose job is to let the dead into the Underworld, but not to let them out again. It is indeed like this once you're in a Pluto transit: you try and carry on as before, and it won't work. In 1994, as Pluto was squaring my Sun, I kept trying to get up and do things, and everything turned messy and painful. That was Kerberos. It was only when I gave up (to some extent) identifying myself with my conscious will and its 'achievements' that things were able to come right.

Tartarus is described as being as far beneath Hades as Earth is beneath the sky. It is so dark that the

"night is poured around it in three rows like a collar round the neck, while above it grow the roots of the earth and of the unharvested sea." (Wikipedia)

I think Tartarus represents deeply repressed aspects of ourselves. That repression is painful. The usual reaction, which is unconscious, is to find ways to avoid that pain. Alcohol and drugs, victimising others, health issues, keeping busy. A Pluto transit, if we're prepared to be aware, brings us to the point where all those diverting strategies are gone, they are dead, taken away from us, and we are just left with the pain that we probably don't understand.

There is no redemption in the Greek Underworld, once you are there that is it, and the other place of suffering, the Fields of Punishment, doesn't seem any better than Tartarus. (Tartarus, however, with its sheer depth beneath Hades, best symbolises repression.)

At this point, where we begin to emerge renewed from the Pluto transit, I think we need to leave the Greek mythology behind, though of course the story of Persephone tells us a certain amount, as do, in a kind of way, the Elysian Fields.

The Underworld is not just a place of suffering. The Elysian Fields are for those who have distinguished themselves. Wikipedia:

> *"Usually, those who had proximity to the gods were granted admission, rather than those who were especially righteous or had ethical merit."*

A Pluto transit is by no means just about dismemberment and suffering (suffering which has often been there all along, but which we have been unconsciously avoiding.) You see some people going from strength to strength under these transits, it is not a deep internal journey. And some seem able to put up with the difficulty and suffering that comes along in the form of external events and then carry on as before.

You also see that while on the one hand some people are feeling dismembered (Tartarus), they are also experiencing an accession of their gifts and talents (Elysian Fields). The gifts that are central to you, but which maybe you and the world haven't sufficiently valued, typically come to the fore during a Pluto transit. In a way, that is what the transit is about: a purging of the old personality to make way for a more authentic self, and the gifts that come with it, whose time has come.

The Elysian Fields are for those who have had proximity to the gods, rather than 'good' people. This says a lot about the process of life changing and moving on. It happens not by being a 'good' person and following the social and religious rules you were born into, though that may get you worldly rewards. It is about sensing what the gods want of you and having the courage to act on that. It is about doing what you 'have' to do.

It is about finding that level in yourself, that is often revealed by Pluto transits, that is a new type of identity: not the easy, unconscious one formed by aligning oneself with social norms and expectations, but something that is purely within you – the Self, the Dreambody, whatever you want to call it, perhaps it's best not to call it anything.

That is what Pluto is really trying to do when he takes us to his Underworld, because that is what Life is trying to do. It is that something, that solid, alive, creative foundation within, that knows how to live and is our true guide. In a way our only task is to be loyal to that, which is also being loyal to the gods and to Pluto.

This is where distinction and the Elysian Fields lie. For ordinary mortals we have the Asphodel Meadows, whose descriptions vary, but in the Odyssey its inhabitants "flit like shadows" and have lost the power of independent thought – but did they truly have it in life?

There is no redemption or transformation within the Greek Underworld, but there is a kind of parallel to the emergence from a Pluto transit, strengthened and renewed, in that those who enter the Elysian Fields have a choice to either stay there or be reborn. If a soul was re-born three times and achieved Elysium each time, then he/she could enter the Isles of the Blessed, and eternal paradise.

Emergence from a Pluto transit is a bit like being re-born from the Elysian Fields, which is for those who have lived close to the gods. You have been touched and changed by a god, and you come back to your life again, but renewed and on a different inner basis.

Finally, there are the rivers of Hades – Styx, Acheron, Lethe, Phlegethon and Cocytus – associated with hatred, pain, oblivion, fire and wailing respectively. The rivers appear in both this world and the Underworld. Wikipedia:

"Their names were meant to reflect the emotions associated with death."

Presumably that means the emotions associated with dying rather than being dead, for otherwise there wouldn't be the Elysian Fields. Psychologically, they partly seem to describe the painful emotions associated with a Pluto transit that is being resisted – and that is often an unconscious thing. It even happens to us good guys who think we are up for change (ha ha! Pluto soon shows us where we are not.)

The rivers are also unacknowledged pain that gets dredged up by Pluto. Rivers of pain: that is the metaphor that the Greek Underworld presents us with. Rivers that flow through us, and we need to go with them downstream to the ocean, to the bigger identity that Pluto is pushing for. Pluto is never just helping us sort our psychological difficulties in a narrow sense. There is always a bigger agenda, a new perspective on ourselves and on existence that is the real meaning of the transit. The Underworld is the place from which we move on to the next stage of life, and our psychological difficulties are a gateway to that. They are like fissures under the earth, represented by Pluto's brother Chiron, through which the molten lava of the outer planets, of life, can break through. Their father Saturn is the guy who has the responsibility for giving shape to the results of all this seismic activity. In this way Saturn and Chiron are each in their own way bridges to the outer planets, as we saw in Chapter 17.

Hatred, pain, oblivion, fire and wailing. A graphic quintet of suffering through which we pass into the Underworld. Oblivion is the forgetting of our previous earthly existence that occurs when we drink from the river Lethe, a requirement for the shades who have entered the Underworld.

"Shades": that is, in a sense, what we can become under a life changing transit, at least for a while. We may go through the motions of day-to-day existence, but our energy has been taken elsewhere for transformation. That is what I often suggest people try to tune into at these difficult times when 'normal' life no longer seems to work. It is as though the energy has all gone into a crucible deep within, and if you can tune into that, you'll see that life is there just as strongly as it was before, but in a different form, a natural form that we are not used to, but which constitutes winter in the myth of Persephone. Like the bulb of a tulip or daffodil, or the chrysalis of a butterfly.

The Oblivion, the Forgetting, is part of this. You may notice, as a Pluto transit begins, that some activity that was very important to you starts to lose its appeal. The energy and interest that were there have leached away, almost without you noticing. This can be very painful if, for example, your sense of who you are, or your livelihood, or your marriage, are involved. But the 'old you' has gone, you have forgotten him/her. And this is necessary in order for the new eventually to be born.

This is always an interesting period – when we are a Shade – because we often can't define ourselves in the usual way. The standard props that make us 'normal' – career, marriage, earnings, reputation – may fall away, and in a way, we are dead to the world. So how do we define ourselves in this period, how do we value ourselves when we have nothing to show?

Pluto humbles us, and we have to look within for a source of value. He is the destroyer of Saturn the worldly taskmaster, who says you are only your earnings and your social standing, that which can be measured. Painful as it is, we can emerge from the Underworld with a looser and more open sense of who we are, with less of a need to define ourselves, and more open therefore to the outer planets, to the gods.

The Pluto transit can also reveal a previous forgetting. For whatever reason – self-doubt, perceived expectations of others, lack of courage, unbalanced sense of values – Pluto's riches, our gifts and talents, can be put to one side, dismissed as nugatory. This can go on right through life. And it often seems to apply to talents that are very particular and personal to us, for which there are no recognised certificates to re-assure us that we are indeed competent. You and you alone have to be the judge of that, you have to find a confidence that is independent of others. And I get this issue regularly in readings, for it is often a stopping point for people, they can go no further unless they go through the fires of self-doubt, which may last for years: that sort of fire almost seems to be part of the initiation into one's own gifts. And into one's individuality, another of Pluto's gifts: that which makes us distinct from the collective, which pursued far enough makes us distinguished, like the beings in the Elysian Fields.

In this sense the function of the transit is to get us to remember that which we have forgotten. Not usually entirely forgotten: sometimes it is like a niggle that we have put to one side, maybe for years or decades, that can seem like a small part of us. But then that niggle turns out, under a Pluto transit, to be something much bigger than we ever thought. All we saw was Chiron, the fissure, and not the molten Plutonian lava underneath. This ignoring can be a like a deep pain that we are sometimes aware of, Tartarus, repressed aspects of ourselves. The river out of Tartarus is Phlegethon, the river of fire that we may need to go through in claiming our gifts.

There can be a make-or-break quality to this encounter with Tartarus. In the words of saying No 70 of the Gospel of St Thomas:

"If you bring forth what is within you, what you bring forth will save you. If you do not bring forth what is within you, what you do not bring forth will destroy you."

But let's move out of the 'psychological' in the sense of a purely inner experience. I don't think Pluto and the Underworld can be fully understood in those terms, for Pluto is a god and the Underworld is a place, and the natural way to understand them therefore is as 'outer' rather than 'inner'. As I said earlier, let us not separate those two categories too rigidly. It is an artificial distinction that is necessary for everyday life.

Under a major Pluto transit (or Neptune for that matter) it

can be as though our soul has gone elsewhere. We can say it has withdrawn deep within, or we can say it has gone somewhere else. We are probably the only society that has ever existed that has a predominant belief that material reality is the only reality, with all the rigidity around space and time that comes with that. For such a mind-set, our personality is confined to and identical with the physical limits of the body. I suspect that not many of my readers believe that. Well, you can't believe that if you are an astrologer, for our art is based on the synchronicities between inner and outer. Reality is subtle and without set boundaries. When I write about him, Pluto often turns up as a presence behind my shoulder. That experience is just as real as the desk I am sitting at.

Under a Pluto transit our soul is called to another place, to the Underworld, that is somewhat like the Greek one. It is 'over there' in some subtle reality, in the Otherworld, if you like. A world in which a few of us almost seem to dwell full-time, or at least be aware of all the time as an ongoing part of who we are, as in a way more real than the very solid material world around us.

There are powers in that place, there are gods which as astrologers we identify as the Greek/Roman gods. And we are 'called' there, or even forced there kicking and screaming, under a major Pluto transit. We 'have' to go there, and if we have sense we do so willingly, albeit with teeth gritted and fingers crossed. And a coin in our mouth!

It is our fate. A narrow notion of an all-powerful 'free-will' is absurd beside this psychic reality. And fate seems to have a much better idea of where our life needs to go than does our so-called free will, particularly at times of major change.

That change is not necessarily rooted in the need for personal, psychological change. It may be just one of those things that life throws at us because that is what life does. Everyone dies, everyone goes to Hades, and that is associated with the five rivers of pain. Even if we are psychologically well-balanced and living according to what our vocation demands, what the gods want of us, painful events can still occur under Pluto transits. Close relatives die, we lose our health and so on. Those outer events may have inner correspondences, or they may not: it is part of the astrologer's art – or the readers of omens – to be able to tell.

I think this idea of the gods – of Pluto and his Underworld – as a kind of fate that informs our lives, connects us to a qualitatively different way of living, that free will alone cannot provide. Fate not just as material laws like physical death, but as any event that has a synchronous quality. Since fate, in the sense of the mysterious purposes of the gods, is much bigger than our personal free will, it makes sense to view our lives more as being directed by the gods than by ourselves. Or by the Unconscious, or just by Life itself.

The astrological chart is a map of the claims, sometimes harmonious and sometimes conflicting, that the gods make on us individually: the chart reveals how unique we are, at the same time as revealing our fate. Wisdom is the awareness of those claims, and the ability to respond to them, and in a way the ability not to question them, to know that the wider purposes involved are beyond one individual's understanding.

As a kind of sop to rationalism, astrologers can be eager to deny that the planets cause events; rather, we sometimes say, they are a synchronous reflection of events in our lives and in the world. But I think this does not do justice to fate. Neptune, for example, caused the storms that obstructed Odysseus on his journey home. This seems clear from the Odyssey.

The planets/gods are more powerful forces in our lives than is our individual will, so it is truer to say the planets cause events than it is to say that we do! Of course, we need not to be rigid about this, but at least let us not allow our philosophy of astrology to be determined by modern notions of rationality – a term which originally meant proportionate, as in 'ratio', rather than dryly logical and 'scientific'.

I think this kind of fate vs free will perspective is needed to have a productive relationship with Pluto and the Underworld. The Underworld is life itself; it is a kind of ever-present nourishment and renewal that we can feel if we are connected to it: it provides the power to live our life as it is right now, and it provides the power to change it when the time comes. That power has its own purposes, that also involve the creative spark of Uranus and the continuous re-imagining of life and the universe that is Neptune.

Also by Barry Goddard

The Medicine Wheel
Maps of Transformation, Wholeness and Balance

978-1-78535-967-5 (Paperback)
978-1-78535-968-2 (ebook)

MOON
BOOKS

PAGANISM & SHAMANISM

What is Paganism? A religion, a spirituality, an alternative
belief system, nature worship? You can find support for all these
definitions (and many more) in dictionaries, encyclopaedias, and
text books of religion, but subscribe to any one and the truth will
evade you. Above all Paganism is a creative pursuit, an encounter
with reality, an exploration of meaning and an expression of the
soul. Druids, Heathens, Wiccans and others, all contribute their
insights and literary riches to the Pagan tradition. Moon Books
invites you to begin or to deepen your own encounter, right here,
right now.
If you have enjoyed this book, why not tell other readers by
posting a review on your preferred book site.

Recent bestsellers from Moon Books are:

Journey to the Dark Goddess
How to Return to Your Soul
Jane Meredith
Discover the powerful secrets of the Dark Goddess and
transform your depression, grief and pain into healing
and integration.
Paperback: 978-1-84694-677-6 ebook: 978-1-78099-223-5

Shamanic Reiki
Expanded Ways of Working with Universal Life Force Energy
Llyn Roberts, Robert Levy
Shamanism and Reiki are each powerful ways of healing; together,
their power multiplies. *Shamanic Reiki* introduces techniques to
help healers and Reiki practitioners tap ancient healing wisdom.
Paperback: 978-1-84694-037-8 ebook: 978-1-84694-650-9

Pagan Portals – The Awen Alone
Walking the Path of the Solitary Druid
Joanna van der Hoeven
An introductory guide for the solitary Druid, *The Awen Alone* will
accompany you as you explore, and seek out your own place
within the natural world.
Paperback: 978-1-78279-547-6 ebook: 978-1-78279-546-9

A Kitchen Witch's World of Magical Herbs & Plants
Rachel Patterson
A journey into the magical world of herbs and plants, filled with
magical uses, folklore, history and practical magic. By popular
writer, blogger and kitchen witch, Tansy Firedragon.
Paperback: 978-1-78279-621-3 ebook: 978-1-78279-620-6

Medicine for the Soul
The Complete Book of Shamanic Healing
Ross Heaven
All you will ever need to know about shamanic healing and how to
become your own shaman...
Paperback: 978-1-78099-419-2 ebook: 978-1-78099-420-8

Shaman Pathways – The Druid Shaman
Exploring the Celtic Otherworld
Danu Forest
A practical guide to Celtic shamanism with exercises and
techniques as well as traditional lore for exploring the Celtic
Otherworld.
Paperback: 978-1-78099-615-8 ebook: 978-1-78099-616-5

Traditional Witchcraft for the Woods and Forests
A Witch's Guide to the Woodland with Guided Meditations and
Pathworking
Mélusine Draco
A Witch's guide to walking alone in the woods, with guided
meditations and pathworking.
Paperback: 978-1-84694-803-9 ebook: 978-1-84694-804-6

Wild Earth, Wild Soul
A Manual for an Ecstatic Culture
Bill Pfeiffer
Imagine a nature-based culture so alive and so connected,
spreading like wildfire. This book is the first flame...
Paperback: 978-1-78099-187-0 ebook: 978-1-78099-188-7

Naming the Goddess
Trevor Greenfield
Naming the Goddess is written by over eighty adherents and
scholars of Goddess and Goddess Spirituality.
Paperback: 978-1-78279-476-9 ebook: 978-1-78279-475-2

Shapeshifting into Higher Consciousness
Heal and Transform Yourself and Our World with Ancient
Shamanic and Modern Methods
Llyn Roberts
Ancient and modern methods that you can use every day to
transform yourself and make a positive difference in the world.
Paperback: 978-1-84694-843-5 ebook: 978-1-84694-844-2

Readers of ebooks can buy or view any of these bestsellers by
clicking on the live link in the title. Most titles are published in
paperback and as an ebook. Paperbacks are available in traditional
bookshops. Both print and ebook formats are available online.

Find more titles and sign up to our readers' newsletter at
http://www.johnhuntpublishing.com/paganism
Follow us on Facebook at https://www.facebook.com/MoonBooks
and Twitter at https://twitter.com/MoonBooksJHP